W9-BLG-988

Instruction for All Students

Strategies

Resources

Rationales

Paula Rutherford

Just ASK Publications, Attitudes, Skills & Knowledge (ASK), Inc.

2214 King Street, Alexandria, VA 22301 1-800-940-5434, Fax 703-535-8502, email: info@askeducation.com

About the Author

Paula Rutherford is an educational consultant specializing in educational leadership, school improvement, instruction, and communication skills. Much of her time is spent in multifaceted and long term work with school districts where leadership and staff are committed to a focus on educating all students and are willing to engage in the hard work necessary to make educational excellence for all a reality. In addition to her extensive work as a consultant and trainer, her experience includes work in regular education K-12 as a teacher of high school history and social sciences, physical education, Spanish, and kindergarten, as well as a special education teacher, coordinator of special education programs, school administrator at the middle school and high school levels, and as a central office staff development specialist.

She may be contacted directly at paula@askeducation.com for training, consulting, or facilitating services.

See the last page for ordering information for this book, *The 21ˢᵗ Century Mentor's Handbook*, *Why Didn't I Learn This in College?* and *Leading the Learning-A Field Guide for Supervisors, Coaches, and Mentors* which were also written by Paula Rutherford.

Instruction for All Students

Published by Just ASK Publications
a division of Attitudes, Skills, and Knowledge, (ASK), Inc.
2214 King Street
Alexandria, Virginia 22301
TOLL FREE 1-800-940-5434
VOICE 1-703-535-5434
FAX 1-703-535-8502
email info@askeducation.com
www.askeducation.com

Printed in the United States of America
ISBN 10: 0-9663336-2-4
ISBN 13: 978-0-9663336-2-6

Instruction for All Students

INSTRUCTION for ALL STUDENTS

Instruction for All Students
Reproducible Black Line Masters

Permission is given purchasers of this book to reproduce the following pages for classroom and planning use. This in no way authorizes duplication for use in workshops or for school or systemwide distribution. Please contact the author for any additional reproduction requests.

Introduction

We will conduct all of our interactions with students based on the most current data, research, and current thinking in our field. When this information changes, we will change our practice.*

This statement in no way implies that we should continue to hop from band wagon to band wagon looking for materials and programs that will ensure quick fixes or successes. Quite the contrary. It means that we must constantly reach out to, analyze, reflect on, and react to the massive body of research on teaching and learning that comes, not only from those doing formal research, but also from those of us working directly with students.

There are three additional ideas that we must come to terms with before we will accomplish all we might. The first is that we and our students have the capacity to achieve far more than we have so far. Ron Edmonds called us to action by saying that whether or not we and our students achieve more depends, to a large extent, on how we feel about the fact that what we've been doing hasn't brought all the results we seek. The second important idea is that we cannot accomplish all we might until we see ourselves as part of a greater whole, and expand our efforts for working collaboratively. The third major component is that we must become much more clearly focused on what we believe students should know and be able to do; then we must focus our time and energy on moving all students toward those goals. It is no longer good enough for the lesson to be a "*good lesson*", it must also be the "*right lesson.*"

This book is based on an analysis of the research base on teaching and learning, and on the work of educators in schools around the world. The ideas presented here have been productive for educators on multiple occasions, but there is absolutely no guarantee that all of the material and ideas will work for you. There is, however, a strong likelihood that we will all accomplish far more if we engage in our practice with:

> ➤ a sense of self-efficacy
> ➤ a focus on clearly articulated standards and objectives
> ➤ an ever growing repertoire of skills for teaching and assessing diverse learners
> ➤ a passion for engaging all students in the learning process
> ➤ the use of data to make and assess instructional decisions
> ➤ a mission to promote high standards and expectations for both students and educators
> ➤ a commitment to collaborate with colleagues and parents

**Source unknown

Acknowledgements

The people who have greatly influenced my thinking about teaching, learning and leading, and who have served as mentors include, but are certainly not limited to, my two sons, Doug and Mike; Clint Van Nagel and Paul Eggen of the University of North Florida; Louise Thompson of Louise Thompson Associates; Jon Saphier, Executive Director of Research for Better Teaching (RBT), as well as all my colleagues in that organization; Kathi Ruh, Executive Director Curriculum and Instruction, East Maine School District #63, DesPlaines, Illinois; Mary Alice Price, superintendent of Pittsford Central Schools, Pittsford, New York; Janie Smith, former Director of High School Instruction and Curriculum, Fairfax County Public Schools, Fairfax, Virginia; Mary Herrmann, Superintendent, Barrington Community Unit School District 220, Barrington, Illinois; and the thousands of educators and students I have had the good fortune to work with in schools and workshops throughout the past thirty plus years.

The teachers who have so willingly shared their expertise and thinking by providing specific examples of strategies that have worked well in their instructional programs are cited by name and school district. They have taught me so much about teaching and learning and truly exemplify the concept of collegial collaboration!

A special thanks goes to the wonderful women who have worked with me as graphic designers and administrative assistants for the five years I wrote and revised, and revised, and revised again. They are Karen Grady, Anna Daley, Margie Spendiker, Valerie Fairchild, Kris Saum, Jennifer Wiley, Connie Phares, and Mary Crohn.

The biggest thanks goes to the person who is president of my fan club and believes in me beyond all reason, my husband, David.

The Big Picture

What educational purposes should the school seek to attain?

How can learning experiences be selected which are likely to be useful in attaining these objectives?

How can learning experiences be organized for effective instruction?

How can the effectiveness of learning experiences be evaluated?

-Ralph Tyler, 1949

The News
...that's Shaping Our Thinking

Do You Hear What We Hear?

performance assessment

differentiation

inclusion

block scheduling

rubrics

standards & proficiencies

self-efficacy

time and learning

collaboration

brain-based learning

thinking as a basic skill

co-curricular

communities of learners

data-driven decisions

instructional technology

repertoire building

Collaborative Practices a Priority

The work of Judith Warren Little, Susan Rosenholtz, and Ann Lieberman has clear implications for the ways in which educators need to interact and collaborate with each other. In schools where collegial practices are the norm, student achievement levels increase dramatically. The literal and figurative walls we have constructed must be removed so that our students can be more successful in school and in life.

Principles of Brain-Based Learning

1. The brain is a complex adaptive system.
2. The brain is a social brain.
3. The search for meaning is innate.
4. The search for meaning occurs through "patterning."
5. Emotions are critical to patterning.
6. The brain simultaneously perceives and creates parts and wholes.
7. Learning involves both focused attention and peripheral perception.
8. Learning always involves conscious and unconscious processing.
9. We have at least two ways of organizing memory.
10. Learning is developmental.
11. Complex learning is enhanced by challenge and inhibited by threat.
12. Each brain is uniquely organized.

Caine and Caine

Brain Research & Theories of Intelligence	SCANS Report & School to Work Initiative

Questions about Teaching, Learning and Assessment

Restructuring Schools including Block Scheduling & Inclusion	National & State Standards

Only when we constantly examine our practices and belief systems can we ensure that *all students DO learn.* We must analyze the effectiveness of past practices and integrate the best of the past with most recent available data.

Major NASSP Report Published

High schools will develop flexible scheduling that allows for more varied uses of time in order to meet the requirements of the core curriculum...*Breaking Ranks*

SCANS
A Blueprint for High Performance

To schools, the SCANS message is *"Look beyond the years students spend in school to the roles students will play when they leave to become workers, parents, and citizens."*

To teachers, the SCANS report suggests *"Look beyond your discipline and your classroom to the other classes your students take, to the community, and to the lives your students lead outside of school. Help your students connect what they learn in class to the world beyond the classroom and school walls."*

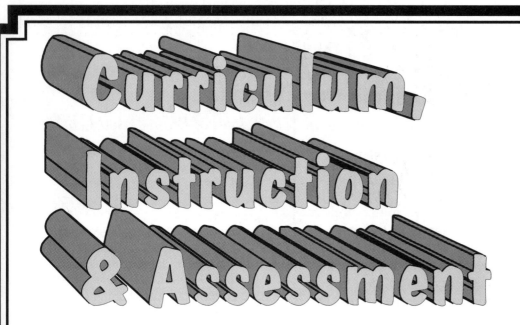

Curriculum: WHAT IS TAUGHT & LEARNED

Curriculum is the structured set of learning outcomes for a prescribed course of study. Most districts have aligned, or are now working to align, their curricula with state and national standards. To ensure that the identified curricula represents consensus about what students need to learn requires much thought and many voices.

Instruction: HOW WE TEACH

Instruction is the repertoire of teaching and learning strategies we use to design experiences that promote student learning of the curriculum. Thoughtful professional educators work throughout their careers to build extensive repertoires so that they can provide varied learning experiences and make purposeful selections to best meet the needs of their learners.

Assessment: HOW WE KNOW WHAT THEY HAVE LEARNED

Assessment is the repertoire of ways we have students demonstrate what they know and what they can do with what they know. Daily activities and assignments provide formative assessment which allow both teachers and learners to make instructional and learning decisions. Both formative and summative assessment are most effective when the tasks are engaging, authentic, and rigorous. Assessment tasks and measures must, of course, be aligned with curriculum and standards.

All students, including special and remedial students, need to learn what is in the curriculum; it is the instructional and assessment methods that may be different. The curriculum is designed to prepare ALL students for successful living in society.

Yesterday & Today...
Where We've Been & Where We Are Going

Curriculum

What is taught	What is learned
Chapters covered and workbooks completed	Identification of what student should know and be able to do
Academic context	Life context
Textbook as resource	Multiple resources
Individual subjects	Integrated subjects
Basics emphasized for all; thinking skills emphasized for gifted	Basics and thinking skills emphasized for all

Instruction

Teacher centered	Learner centered
Organized around time	Organized for results
Single teaching strategy	Multiple teaching strategies
Teach once	Reteaching and enrichment
Fixed groups	Flexible groups
Whole group instruction	Differentiated instruction
Passive learning	Active learning

Assessment

Bell curve	Public and precise criteria
One opportunity	Multiple opportunities
After instruction	Integrated with instruction
Paper and pencil based	Performance based
Grades averaged	Standard met or not met
Proving and accountability	Diagnose and prescribe
Focus on product	Focus on product and process

BREAKING RANKS:
Changing An American Institution

High Schools must...

☐ be **learning communities** committed to expecting academic achievement from every student

☐ provide **transitional experiences** during which all students are prepared for the next stage of their lives, whether it is further formal education or the work force, with the acknowledgement that eventually all students will need to support themselves financially

☐ prepare all students for a **life of learning**

☐ give students the tools to be **good citizens** and active participants in a democracy

☐ include experiences that meet the **social needs** of students in order to promote their personal development

☐ prepare students to live and work in a highly **technological world**

☐ build in students a capacity to thrive in a **diverse country and world** where acceptance and collaboration with others who are quite different from them is a basic skill

☐ **be advocates** for youth

Breaking Ranks: Changing an American Institution: **A Report of the National Association of Secondary School Principals on the high school of the 21st century. 1996**

BLOCK SCHEDULING
What are the Opportunities for My Students & for Me?

- ☐ to use and benefit from a variety of **instructional strategies**

- ☐ to include more meaningful and **active learning experiences**

- ☐ to explore **key concepts** in depth

- ☐ to create a more **personalized school environment**

- ☐ to integrate **technology** into the curriculum

- ☐ to develop higher level **thinking skills**

- ☐ to **differentiate** instruction and learning

- ☐ to design and use a variety of **assessment strategies**

- ☐ to do more **interdisciplinary** teaching and learning

- ☐ to **interact** with fewer students (teachers) and fewer courses per day

- ☐ to have more **uninterrupted** planning, teaching, and learning **time**

Restructuring time is one significant way secondary educators are attempting to meet the criteria laid out in *Breaking Ranks*. Extended instructional periods make sense in many instances because of the opportunities described above. If your secondary school is on a "traditional" schedule, your task is to rethink how you use time in that setting and how you might reconfigure the instructional program to accomplish more of the criteria cited in *Breaking Ranks*. Elementary teachers are masters at using different chunks of time throughout the school day and year, so they are excellent resources to secondary teachers interested in restructuring time allocation.

SCANS
A THREE PART FOUNDATION

Reading
Writing
Arithmetic/Mathematics
Listening
Speaking

Creative Thinking
Decision Making
Problem Solving
Seeing Things in the Mind's Eye
Knowing How to Learn

Responsibility
Self-Esteem
Sociability
Self-Management
Integrity/Honesty

SCANS FIVE COMPETENCIES

Resources

Time
Money
Material and Facilities
Human Resources

*Identifies,
Organizes,
& Allocates*

Information

Acquires and Evaluates
Organizes and Maintains
Interprets and Communicates
Uses Computers to Process

Systems

Understands Systems
Monitors and Corrects Performance
Improves or Designs Systems

*Organizational,
Social, and/or
Technological*

Technology

Selects Technology
Applies Technology to Task
Maintains and Troubleshoots Equipment

Interpersonal

Teaches Others New Skills
Serves Clients/Customers
Exercises Leadership/Persuasion
Negotiates
Works with Diversity
Participates as Member of a Team

Standards Based Education

States and districts continue the effort to define and refine the standards of learning that their students are to achieve. Certain patterns are emerging as the "bar is raised" for teaching and learning in our schools. The following commonalties are present across the country:

- State and/or district standards drive **curriculum planning** and **classroom decisions**.

- **Results of assessment** are used by educators **to plan future instruction** because they provide data about the effectiveness of past instruction in moving students toward the standards.

- The **focus** is on **what students have learned** rather than on what the teacher has covered.

- The **standards apply to all students**, even those who in the past have not been held to high standards and to those who have a history of performing at low levels.

- Since "One size does not fit all," teachers must **differentiate instruction** in order to move more students toward competency with the standards.

Writing standards of learning is just one of the steps we need to take to move toward higher achievement by more students. Whether or not the standards movement has a lasting impact on the learning of America's children depends on several additional variables.

These include whether or not teachers, students, and other interested stakeholders:

- reach consensus on what is absolutely **essential for all students to know and be able to do**

- believe in the significance of having standards and **focusing instruction and assessment on content standards**

- understand how the **standards and course content are related**

- believe that **students are capable** of achieving the standards

- can accept the fact that learning is the constant and that **time is the variable**

- have the **courage to stay the course** when all students are not successful the first, or even the second, time around.

Standards Based Education continued...

Additionally, it depends on whether or not teachers:

- ▣ are committed to creating a clear and **direct relationship between the standards and each lesson**, assignment, project, and assessment

- ▣ can collaborate to identify, and reach consensus around, **clearly articulated performance levels**

- ▣ build capacity and commitment to providing support and **adaptations for special needs students**

- ▣ are willing and able to use **multiple resources and strategies**, including technology, as instructional tools

- ▣ create a classroom atmosphere that promotes a supportive and **emotionally safe learning community**

- ▣ provide opportunities for **student choice and decision making** around issues that really matter

- ▣ develop expertise at designing **multiple formats of assessment** and at establishing **clear criteria for performance** for each

- ▣ become proficient at using **classroom, district, state, and national data to make instructional decisions**

- ▣ have the courage to continue to **believe in their own capacity** and **the capacity of their students** when the data is analyzed.

And, it depends on whether or not students, as developmentally appropriate:

- ▣ develop a working **knowledge of the standards of learning**, the assessment, and the assessment criteria

- ▣ **monitor their own learning** and the effectiveness of their effort

- ▣ **evaluate their own work,** prior to teacher evaluation, using the same criteria the teacher will use

- ▣ **set goals** and create **action plans** to accomplish those goals

- ▣ **analyze data** generated in the classroom and at the district, state, and national level to **generate personal learning plans.**

Lesson
& Unit
Design

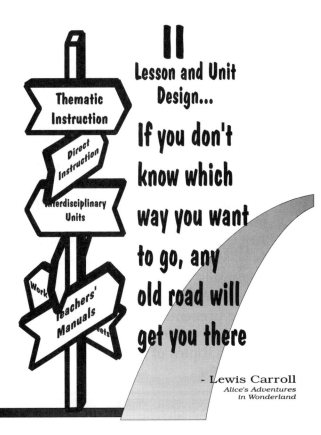

II
Lesson and Unit Design...

If you don't know which way you want to go, any old road will get you there

- Lewis Carroll
Alice's Adventures in Wonderland

Thematic Instruction

Direct Instruction

Interdisciplinary Units

Work... Teachers' Manuals ...ets

Planning Instruction for the Year

All decisions are based on district standards combined with your knowledge of the DISCIPLINE(S) you teach and of the STUDENTS who are to learn this curriculum.

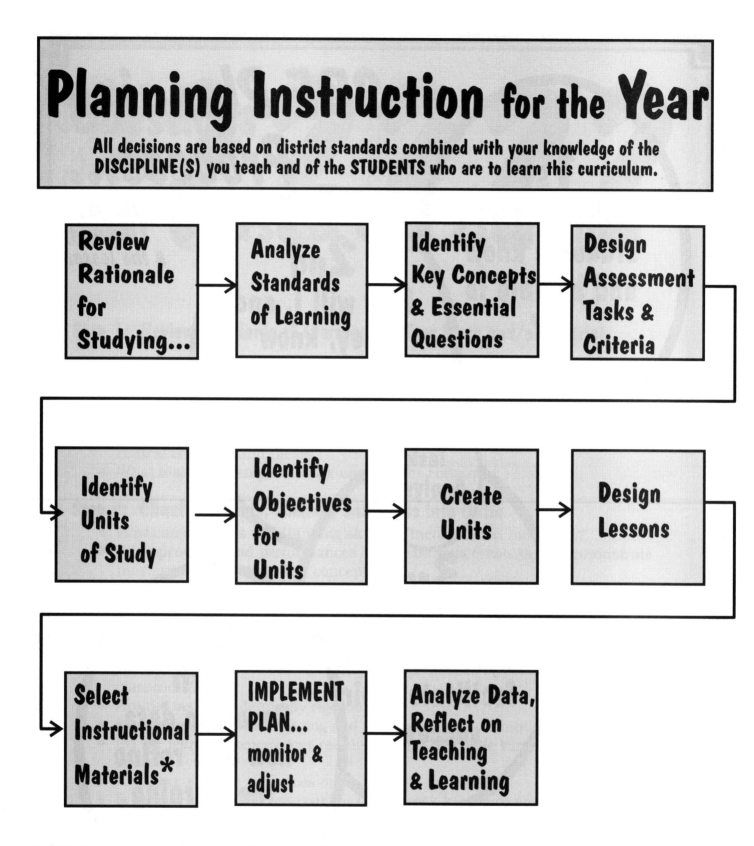

Review Rationale for Studying... → Analyze Standards of Learning → Identify Key Concepts & Essential Questions → Design Assessment Tasks & Criteria

Identify Units of Study → Identify Objectives for Units → Create Units → Design Lessons

Select Instructional Materials* → IMPLEMENT PLAN... monitor & adjust → Analyze Data, Reflect on Teaching & Learning

* "Select Instructional Materials" is placed at this point in the sequence because the focus must be on teaching to the standards of learning in ways that match the students needs, interests, and backgrounds rather than how much time to spend on each chapter in the textbook. The textbook can be a valuable tool but we must remember that we teach students not textbooks!

TOP TEN QUESTIONS
to ask myself as I design LESSONS

1st What should **students know and be able to do** with what they know as a result of this lesson? How are these objectives related to national, state, and/or district standards or proficiencies?

2nd How will **students demonstrate what they know and what they can do?** What multiple forms of assessment including **self assessment** can I use? What will be the **assessment criteria** and what form will it take?

3rd Questions 3 -10 address the third step of the SBE Planning Process.

3. How will **I find out** what **students already know (preassessment),** and how will I help them access what they know and have experienced both inside and outside the classroom? How will **I help them** not only **build on prior experiences,** but **deal with misconceptions** and reframe their thinking when appropriate?

4. How will new knowledge, concepts, and skills be introduced? Given the **diversity** of my students and my **task analysis**, what are **my best options for sources and presentation modes** of new material?

5. How will **I facilitate student processing (meaning making)** of new information or processes? What are the key questions, activities, and assignments (in class or homework)?

6. How will **I check for student understanding** during the lesson?

7. What do I need to do to **differentiate instruction** so that the learning experiences are productive for all students?

8. How will I **"Frame the Learning"** so that **students know the objectives**, the **rationale** for the objectives and activities, the directions and procedures, as well as the **assessment criteria** at the beginning of the learning process?

9. How will I build in opportunities for students to make **real world connections** and to learn and use **varied and complex thinking skills**?

10. What adjustments need to be made in the **learning environment** and in **instruction** so that all students can work and learn efficiently? How is **data** being used to make these decisions?

Worksheet for The TOP TEN QUESTIONS to ask myself as I design LESSONS

1st Step

1. What should **students know and be able to do** with what they know as a result of this lesson? How are these objectives related to national, state, and/or district **standards**? How are these objectives related to the **big ideas/key concepts** of the course?

2nd Step

2. How will **students demonstrate what they know and what they can do** with what they know? What multiple forms of assessment including **self assessment** can I use? What will be the **assessment criteria** and what form will it take? See pages 147-171.

TOP TEN QUESTIONS WORKSHEET CONTINUED...

3rd Step: Questions 3 - 10 address the 3rd Step.

3. How will I find out what **students already know (preassessment),** and how will I help them access what they know and have experienced both inside and outside the classroom? How will **I help them** not only **build on prior experiences,** but **deal with misconceptions** and **reframe their thinking** when appropriate? See pages 73-11.

4. How will new knowledge, concepts, and skills be introduced? Given the diversity of my students and my **task analysis**, what are **my best options for sources and presentation modes** of new material? See pages 49-71.

TOP TEN QUESTIONS WORKSHEET CONTINUED...

5. How will **I facilitate student processing (meaning making)** of new information or processes? What are the key questions, activities, and assignments (in class or homework)? See pages 113-145.

6. How will **I check for student understanding** during the lesson? See pages 108-111.

7. What do I need to do to **differentiate instruction** so that the learning experiences are productive for all students? See pages 189-215.

TOP TEN QUESTIONS WORKSHEET

8. How will I **"Frame the Learning"** so that **students know the objectives**, the **rationale** for the objectives and activities, the directions and procedures, as well as the **assessment criteria** at the beginning of the learning process? See pages 52-53 and 115.

9. How will I build in opportunities for students to make **real world connections** and to learn and use the **varied and complex thinking skills** they need to succeed in the classroom and the world beyond? See pages 129-134, 173-187 and 217-247.

10. What adjustments need to be made in the **learning environment** so that we can work and learn efficiently in a positive and productive classroom setting? How is **data** being used to make these decisions? See pages 259-267.

Materials to be Gathered or Prepared

Timeline/Sequence for Lesson

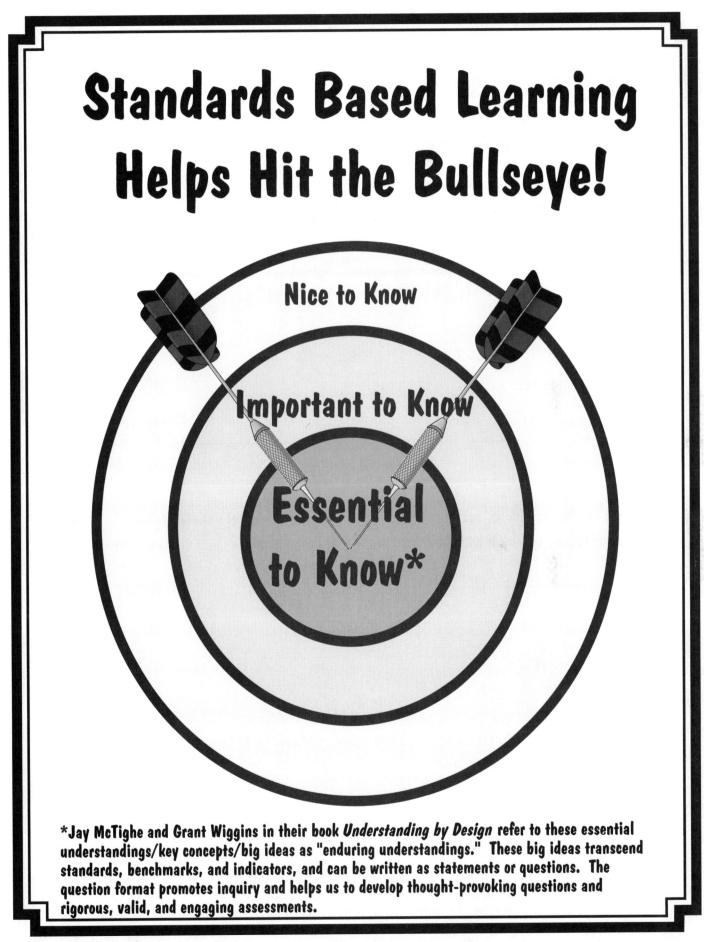

Standards Based Learning Helps Hit the Bullseye!

Nice to Know

Important to Know

Essential to Know*

*Jay McTighe and Grant Wiggins in their book *Understanding by Design* refer to these essential understandings/key concepts/big ideas as "enduring understandings." These big ideas transcend standards, benchmarks, and indicators, and can be written as statements or questions. The question format promotes inquiry and helps us to develop thought-provoking questions and rigorous, valid, and engaging assessments.

A Guide & Worksheet for
Unit Design
in the Standards-Based Classroom

1st STEP: What should students know and be able to do?

1. On which content standard(s)* will the students be working?

2. What are the key ideas, major themes, big concepts or essential understandings embedded in, or which transcend, the standards listed above?

3. Given the essential to know key concepts and ideas identified in #2 how will this unit be different from what/how I taught and asked students to do in years past? If this is a new unit, skip this question.

*Because there are several terms used to designate what we want students to know and be able to do, the term "STANDARDS" is used here as shorthand for whatever your state/district calls the learning goals whether it be standards, benchmarks, indicators, learning outcomes, proficiencies, or something else.

Unit Design in the
Standards-Based Classroom continued...

4. When and where (inside and outside of school) have the students encountered information about and had experience with these key concepts/big ideas before? (Think horizontally and vertically across the curriculum.)

2nd STEP: How will I, and they, know when they are successful?

5. What would it look like when students can demonstrate that they understand the big ideas and have the essential skills? That is, what are some ways they might demonstrate their capacity to use the newly learned concepts/information appropriately in a new situation? (This is a brainstorming opportunity.)

Unit Design in the Standards-Based Classroom continued...

6. What task/products would best demonstrate student understanding? See pages 129-134, 175-185, 154-158. Should I use a rubric or a performance task list, and what criteria should be included? See pages 159-167.

7. What does a task analysis reveal about the skills, the knowledge, and the level of understanding required by the task? See pages 193-194.

8. Do I already have sufficient preassessment data or do I need to gather more? If so, what method shall I use? What does the preassessment data tell me about the skills and knowledge on which the entire group will need to focus? Are there individual students who will need additional support if they are to have a realistic opportunity to demonstrate mastery? In which areas will they need support? See pages 193-194.

Unit Design in the Standards-Based Classroom continued...

3rd STEP: What learning experiences will facilitate their success?

9. How will I "Frame the Learning" so that students know what they are going to be doing, what they will know and be able to do as a result of those activities, how they will be assessed, and how everything they are doing is aligned with the standards? See page 52.

10. How will I help students access prior knowledge and use it productively, either building on it or reframing their thinking as appropriate? See pages 80-107.

Unit Design in the
Standards-Based Classroom continued...

11. What methods of presentation and what active learning experiences can I use to help students achieve the standard? Could I provide multiple sources of information and exercises that would help all students make real world connections and use sophisticated thinking skills? See pages 53-71, 79-107, and 218-247.

12. What assignments, projects, and homework will help students see the relevance of the learning, and help them not only meet the standard but retain their learning? How might I provide multiple pathways to learning? See pages 113-145 and 195-212.

13. What classroom activities/observations, as well as formative quizzes and tests, would provide me and my students information on their progress toward the standard? See pages 108-111, 151-153, and 224-227.

Unit Design in the Standards-Based Classroom continued...

14. What materials and resources do I need to locate and organize to provide multiple pathways to learning? How should I organize the classroom and the materials to provide easy student access?

15. What else might I do to to provide challenging and meaningful experiences for both struggling and advanced learners? Are there other human, print or electronic resources I might consult to refine/review my plan?

Unit Design in the
Standards-Based Classroom continued...

4th STEP: Based on data, how do I refine the learning experiences and/or the assessment?

16. How did students do on the performance task? Were there some students who were not successful? What might account for that? What might I do differently next time? (THIS IS A REALLY IMPORTANT QUESTION!)

17. What else do I need to consider in my advance planning the next time I am focusing on this standard?

Unit Design in the
Standards-Based Classroom continued...

18. Did all of the activities guide students toward mastery of the standard? Are there activities that need to be added, modified, or eliminated? Am I using these activities because I have always used them, or have I analyzed them to be sure that they are the most effective and efficient tools at my disposal?

19. Over all, was this unit effective for addressing the standard(s)? Are there other standards that I could incorporate into this unit, or are there other units of study where I can have the students revisit these standards or essential understandings?

adapted from the Facilitator's Guide and Workbook for *Common Ground in the Standards-Based Education Classroom* prepared by the Northern Colorado BOCES SBE Design Team

Standards-Based Instruction Planning/Analysis Matrix

Standard	Assignment #1	Assignment #2	Assignment #3	Assignment #4	Traditional Assessment	Performance Assessment
Indicator #1						
Indicator #2						
Indicator #3						
Indicator #4						
Indicator #5						
Indicator #6						
Indicator #7						
Indicator #8						

Use this matrix to analyze current units or to plan future units. Cross reference each component of the unit with subsets of the standards to ensure a high correlation. Make necessary adjustments before, during and after instruction.

Approaches to ...
Integrating the Curriculum
In Lesson and Unit Design

Side by Side Two or more content area teachers examine their curriculums to identify broad concepts, as well as social skills and thinking skills, that could be taught simultaneously in both/all classes. Topics or units of study are rearranged and sequenced to coincide with one another. Similar ideas and skills are taught at the same time although the courses remain totally separate classes.

For example, an English teacher might have students read **The Diary of Anne Frank** while they are studying WWII in their history class. Additionally, the two teachers might agree to focus on inductive thinking or on conflict resolution skills during the first quarter of the semester.

That's What Friends Are For Two or more teachers identify concepts and skills that are taught in both/all courses. Through collaborative planning teachers organize lessons that can be taught by one of the teachers, perhaps to quite large groups of students at one time.

For example, formatting of bibliographies, use of graphic organizers, problem solving, consensus building, and communication skills are taught and re-taught across the curriculum. With just a little communication, teacher energy and time, learning could be maximized; and groups of teachers could be freed up to collaborate in the design of future learning experiences or to examine student work.

We Are Family Entire grade level teams, departments or entire schools identify a theme around which teaching and learning can be organized. Elementary teachers are often masters of this because they each teach many curriculums and quite naturally build bridges between what sometimes seems like totally fragmented subject areas.

We Are Family continued...

To organize instruction around a theme, a high school could decide to design a unit around a significant anniversary of the school, around an issue of current importance in the community or the world, around the arts, etc., while an elementary school might focus on habitats, space exploration, or conservation. Concepts such as justice, conflict, fitness, or diversity are also possible areas of focus. It is important to identify key concepts and skills of each curricular area included in the thematic unit so that those important components do not get lost in the energy and excitement generated by the integrated study.

I Heard It Through the Grapevine

In this approach, the learner is bombarded with a selected big idea no matter where he or she turns. Teachers identify and weave thinking skills, social skills, multiple intelligences, technology, or study skills across all the course offerings and co-curricular events of this school.

For example, the staff might identify analytical thinking skills as the focus for a particular time period. Each department/teacher would identify ways to emphasize those skills in their instructional program. Once the areas of focus are identified, individual teachers need only look for opportunities to reinforce the identified skills and explicitly reference their usefulness in this setting, throughout the academic day and in life beyond school.

Theme from 2001

In this **"Go for the Gold"** model, courses, teachers, and students are integrated. This interdisciplinary approach matches subjects or overlaps in topics and concepts with team teaching in an authentic integrated model.

Courses entitled "Humanities" that frequently feature a combination of English, social sciences, and fine arts are examples of a team-taught interdisciplinary course. The multiple intelligences video series from ASCD demonstrates how science, social studies and English can be integrated in a powerful learning situation.

An Integration of the Curriculum Planning Matrix

	Sept.	Oct.	Nov.	Dec.	Jan.	Feb.	Mar.	Apr.	May	June
English										
Fine Arts										
Foreign Language										
History/ Soc. Studies										
Math										
Science										
Phys. Ed/ Health										
Technology Ed.										
Other										

Unit Design
Brainstorming Map

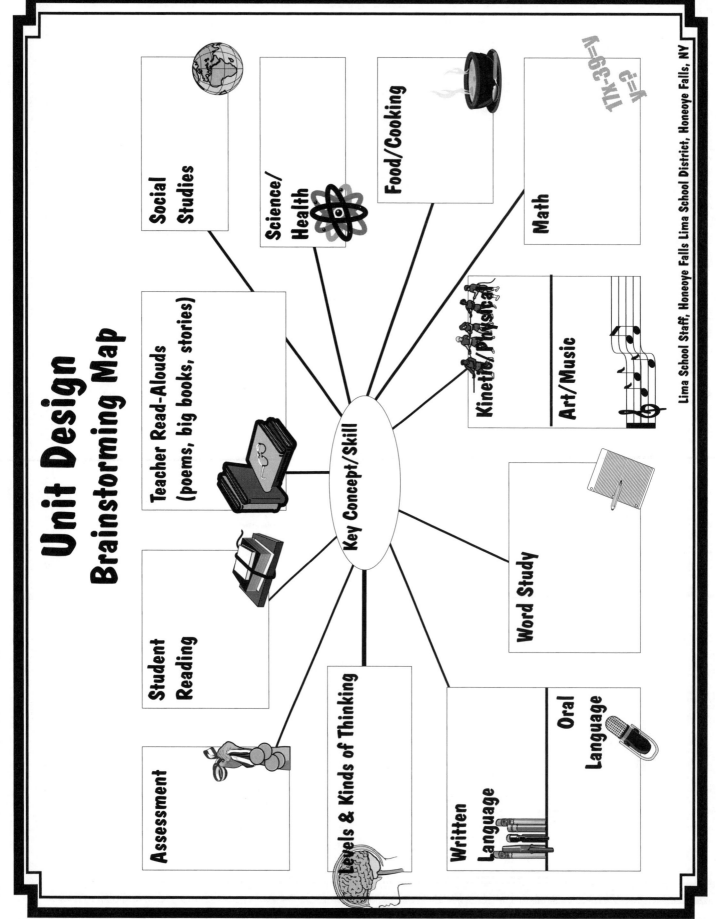

Social Studies

Science/ Health

Food/Cooking

Math

Teacher Read-Alouds (poems, big books, stories)

Key Concept/Skill

Kinetic/Physical

Art/Music

Student Reading

Word Study

Assessment

Levels & Kinds of Thinking

Written Language

Oral Language

Lima School Staff, Honeoye Falls Lima School District, Honeoye Falls, NY

Using the SCANS Report
for Lesson Design

A Three Part Foundation:

Basic Skills	Thinking Skills	Personal Qualities
Reading	Creative Thinking	Responsibility
Writing	Decision Making	Self-Esteem
Mathematics	Problem Solving	Sociability
Listening	Seeing Things in the Mind's Eye	Self-Management
Speaking	Knowing How to Learn	Integrity/Honesty

Five Competencies:

Resources
Time
Money
Material and Facilities
Human Resources

Information
Acquires and Evaluates
Organizes and Maintains
Interprets and Communicates
Uses Computers to Process

Systems
Understands Systems
Monitors and Corrects Performance
Improves or Designs Systems

Technology
Selects Technology
Applies Technology to Task
Maintains and Troubleshoots
    Equipment

Interpersonal
Teaches Others New Skills
Serves Clients/Customers
Exercises Leadership/Persuasion
Negotiates
Works with Diversity
Participates as Member of a Team

SCANS
Lesson Analysis & Planning Guide

Plan/assess units, assignments, and projects for meaning beyond the classroom. A focus on the skills, personal qualities and competencies cited in the SCANS report facilitates that work.

Subject:

Standards being Addressed:

Essential Understandings:

Competency with Resources

Interpersonal Competency

Competency with Information

Competency with Systems

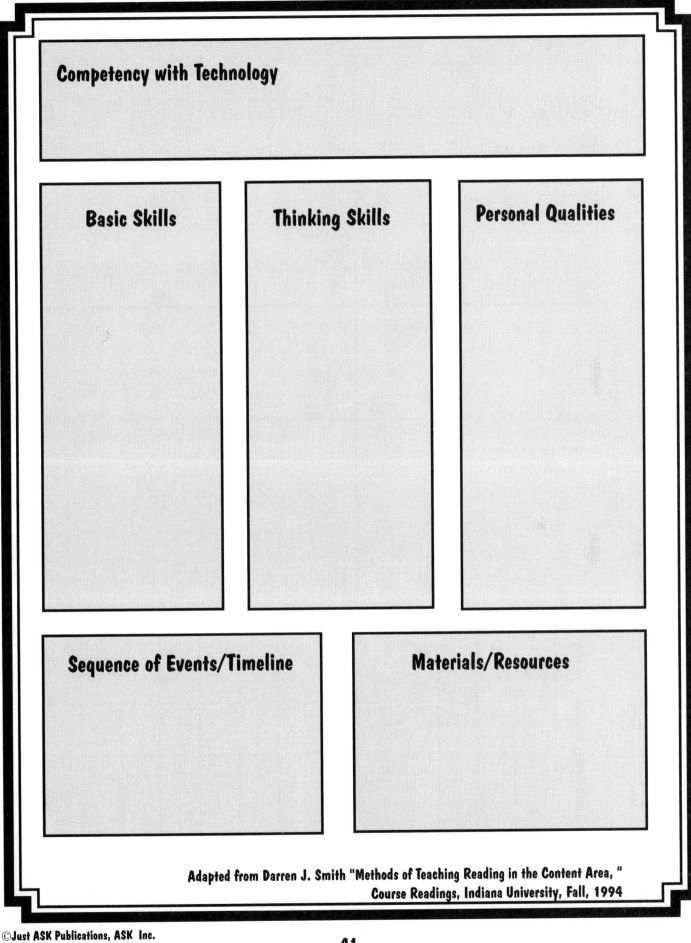

Competency with Technology

Basic Skills

Thinking Skills

Personal Qualities

Sequence of Events/Timeline

Materials/Resources

Adapted from Darren J. Smith "Methods of Teaching Reading in the Content Area, "
Course Readings, Indiana University, Fall, 1994

Multiple Intelligences Unit Planning Sheet

Possible activities for each intelligence:

Logical/ Mathematical	Linguistic/ Verbal	Bodily/ Kinesthetic	Naturalist
Visual/Spatial	Musical/ Rhythmic	Intrapersonal	Interpersonal

Standards, Benchmarks, or Indicators to be Addressed

Key Concepts, Big Ideas, Essential Understandings

Lesson and Unit Design using Multiple Intelligences

Use these questions to plan lessons and units:

1. How might I have the students process information by reading, writing, speaking, and listening? How might I ensure that students use a balance of these four communication skills?

2. How might I teach students to process information and demonstrate learning through the use of numbers, calculations, logic, classifications, and patterns?

3. How might I use color, art, and graphs to explain key concepts? How might I have students process information or demonstrate learning through visualization, graphs, color, art, manipulatives, or metaphors?

4. How might I have students process information through rhythms, patterns of sound, and mnemonics? How can I incorporate music or environmental sounds to create a mood or make a point?

5. How might I have students process information and demonstrate learning through movement and dramatics? What "hands-on" experiences might I include?

6. How might I help students learn to use effective collaboration and communication skills in learning and working situations? How might I have students demonstrate and assess their learning and the effectiveness of their efforts in collaborative situations?

7. How might I promote reflection and metacognition? How might I include multiple opportunities for goal setting and self-assessment?

8. How might I bring the outdoors and nature into the learning environment?

Lesson Design using...
Direct Instruction

Rosenshine (1987) states that the explicit teaching or direct instruction format can be a useful approach when the objective is **skill-building or memorization of a body of knowledge**. He reports that research indicates students need to achieve an **80% success rate during initial practice.**

1. Previous work is **checked and reviewed.**

2. Teacher states **objectives** of the lesson and the **purposes** of the activities.

3. Teacher **explains** concepts or operations and gives **examples** and/or **demonstrates**. Information is presented in **small chunks.**

4. Teacher **checks student understanding** after **each** small chunk of information.

5. Students **practice with guidance** through direct monitoring, feedback, correction, help and hints from the teacher.

6. Students **practice alone** (seatwork or homework).

7. Teacher **re-teaches as needed** to those students who need additional information and/or alternative instruction in order to build identified skills.

8. Teacher gives **frequent tests.**

9. Teacher **reviews** frequently.

Used in isolation, this method can yield misleading test results. Some students can regurgitate information or perform the skills in a contrived setting without having made any sense or meaning of their "learning." This often leads to forgetting, frustration (for both the teacher and the learners), and the need to "teach" the same information over and over again...year after year! It is essential that all skill-building leads to meaningful and engaging work within the same unit of study.

Madeline Hunter's Elements of Lesson Design

Madeline Hunter always described these components as **VARIABLES TO BE CONSIDERED in lesson design**; she never indicated that all lessons should have all of these elements. Hunter's elements, as outlined below, are one **application of the direct instruction model.** The **three categories of decisions** she identified (1982) as components of a teacher's planning of any lesson are:

a.   **what content to teach next**
b.   **what the student will do in order to learn and to demonstrate that the desired learning has occurred**
c.   **what the teacher will do to facilitate that learning**

1.	**Anticipatory Set**	What might I do to focus the attention of the students on the concepts we are about to study?
2.	**Communicate Objectives**	How shall I let students know what it is that they are to know and be able to do? How will I let them know why it is worth knowing?
3.	**Input**	What new content, concepts, information, and skills are to be studied?
4.	**Modeling**	How shall I present/explain the new skill or content?
5.	**Checking for Understanding**	How will I know if and when the students are learning the new information?
6.	**Guided Practice**	How will I help the students practice the new skills with immediate feedback and corrections in class?
7.	**Independent Practice**	What assignments and homework shall I have the students complete to facilitate long-term retention?

Lesson Design using...
Cooperative Learning

- ## Big Picture Decisions
  What are the academic objectives for the lesson?
  What sources will be used to provide essential information about key concepts?
  What are the social skill/group process objectives?
  What cooperative learning model shall I use?

  Learning Together and Alone (Johnson and Johnson)

  Students Teams Achievement Division-STAD (Slavin)

  Team Games Tournament-TGT (Slavin)

  Jigsaw (Aronson, Gonzales)

  Jigsaw II (Slavin)

  Group Investigation (Thelen, Sharon)

- ## Group Composition Decisions
  How many students should be in each group?
  How should the groups be formed?

  Random(number off, draw cards, etc.)

  Heterogeneous by past performance (STAD and TGT, and perhaps other models)

  Heterogeneous by learning/information processing style

  Interest

  Student self selection

- ## Group Interdependence Decisions
  Should roles be assigned to group members? If so, what roles?
  How should positive group interdependence be structured?

  One product/performance/paper from each group

  Randomly selected spokesperson from each group

  Group reward for standards (academic and/or social) achieved by all members of the group

  Each group member earns bonus points if whole group achieves a minimum score or overall average

  Group points for individual members improvement over own previous scores/averages

  One set of materials to share

  Limit time for task (One person would not be able to do task within that time limit.)

  Each member has only part of the information

  Other

  How will I communicate the forms of interdependence and the rationale for the decisions to the students?

Cooperative Learning continued...

- ## Individual Accountability Decisions

  What forms of individual accountability should be used?
  > **All group members sign off**
  > **Individual quizzes**
  > **Individual tests**
  > **Random selection of one paper from group for grading**
  > **Random oral quiz**
  > **Individual homework or products as follow-up**
  > **Other**

  How will I communicate to students, at the beginning of the work, how they are expected to work and to demonstrate learning?
  Should I use a rubric or a task performance list?

- ## Social Skills/Group Process Decisions

  Given the social skills objective, which social skills/group process skills do students need to have mastered? Do we need to review/reflect on past work? What social skills/group skills do I want students to develop?
  How will I communicate the social skills focus? Do I need to model, role play, or develop a see and hear chart?

- ## Assessment and Processing Decisions

  Is assessment beyond what is planned for individual accountability necessary? If so, what needs to be assessed? Should I use a rubric or task performance list?
  How will data be collected for assessment of social skills/group process growth?
  > **Informal observations by teacher**
  > **Informal observations by students**
  > **Formal observations by teacher**

  How will individuals and groups give, receive, and reflect on feedback?
  > **Small or large group debriefing**
  > **Self and group evaluation forms**
  > **Teacher feedback orally or in writing**
  > **Journal and Learning Log entries**

Adapted from Mary Ann Haley

Presentation Modes

TOP TEN QUESTIONS
to ask myself as I design lessons

1. What should **students know and be able to do** with what they know as a result of this lesson? How are these objectives related to national, state, and/or district standards or proficiencies?

2. How will **students demonstrate what they know and what they can do** with what they know? What will be the **assessment criteria** and what form will it take?

3. How will I find out what students already know, and how will I help them access what they know and have experienced both inside and outside the classroom? How will I help them not only build on prior experiences but deal with misconceptions and reframe their thinking when appropriate?

4. How will new knowledge, concepts, and skills be introduced? Given the diversity of my students, what are my best options for sources and presentation modes of new material?

5. How will **I facilitate student processing (meaning making)** of new information or processes? What are the key questions, activities, and assignments (in class or homework)?

6. How will **I check for student understanding** during the lesson?

7. What do I need to do to **differentiate instruction** so that the learning experiences are productive for all students?

8. How will I "Frame the Learning" so that students know the objectives, the rationale for the objectives and activities, the directions and procedures, as well as the assessment criteria at the beginning of the learning process?

9. How will I build in opportunities for students to make **real world connections** and to learn and use the **varied and complex thinking skills** they need to succeed in the classroom and the world beyond?

10. What adjustments need to be made in the **learning environment** so that we can work and learn efficiently during this study?

Presentation Modes

The **"Old Faithfuls"** for the presentation of information to students include lectures, discussions, demonstrations, and printed text. These modes of information are extremely useful when used in balance with other techniques, and when used in a way that promotes student interaction with the information. Most of us have not had formal instruction in the design and implementation of these **"Old Faithfuls"** but have, rather modeled our practice after that of our own teachers. Only recently have teachers widely studied such powerful strategies as the Socratic Seminar or Paideia Seminar. Much valuable guidance has been provided in the reading literature about giving purpose for reading, providing graphic organizers, and designing connection making questions and examples, unfortunately, most of us have had only one three hour course, if any at all, in the teaching of reading. Our exposure to those important findings has been severely limited and we have not been explicitly asked to apply, or been guided in the application of, those strategies to presentation modes beyond the printed text. Given the strength of learning theory through the ages and the power of the current brain research, we need to use both the old and new methods to help us ensure that when we use lectures, discussions, demonstrations, and the printed text we do so in ways that promote the transfer and retention of the learning.

No matter what mode of presentation we select, we need to **Frame the Learning** so that students recognize connections to past learning and experiences, so that they can make new connections as a result of the current learning experiences, and so that they can see the connectedness among the standards of learning, the activities in which they are engaged, and the assessments they are asked to complete.

This chapter provides guidance on how to use the tried and true presentation modes and on how to **Frame the Learning** so that students focus on and retain essential to know concepts and build skills that enable them to not only score well on standardized tests, but to function well in society. See chapters four through nine for additional presentation modes that include students teaching each other, strategies to promote a wide range of thinking skills, and strategies for differentiation of instruction.

Old Faithfuls

Lectures

Demonstrations

Discussions

Readings

Videos

Guest Speakers

Framing the Learning

- **Communicate Standards, the Learning Process & Assessment by**
  - explaining what students need to know & be able to do
  - clarifying why students need to know & be able to do what the standard targets
  - delineating the activities & assessments students will experience in order to process their learning
  - articulating how students will demonstrate learning & the criteria to be used for assessment
  - providing models for processes & products

- **Provide the Agenda/Outline for the Day, Unit & Year**

- **Identify Student Misconceptions & Help Students Reframe Their Thinking**

- **Help Students Access Prior Knowledge & Make Connections**
  - to past experiences both inside & outside of school
  - between concepts/activities at transitions
  - to future areas of study & to life beyond the classroom

- **Have Students Process, Summarize & Use Learning in Meaningful Ways Which Promote Retention & Transfer**

Framing the Learning for...
Readings, Lectures, Demonstrations Multimedia Presentations, Field Trips & Guest Speakers

In the Beginning: Making Connections
- Help students recall what they know about the topic to be studied and/or where they have used or learned related information.
- Have students make predictions about the content and give rationales for their predictions.
- Work with students to set purposes for study and to generate questions to be answered during the lesson.

Presentation of New Information
...via text, videotape, field trip or guest speaker
- Process/summarize at meaningful points. **(Practice 10:2 Theory.)**
- Assess old predictions, make new predictions, and/or identify significant information at the processing points.
- Relate new information to prior knowledge.
- Collaboratively generate more questions throughout the lesson.

Wrapping Up: Connection Making and Locking It In
- Process/summarize the whole lesson.
- Evaluate predictions.
- Return to the purposes set for study to see if they were accomplished; identify additional information that would be interesting or helpful.

Implementation Tips:
- These **"making connections" components** are important at the beginning of new units of study, throughout units to build bridges between fragmented segments, and at the close of lessons and units. **Do not rush to cover material without having students pause for processing!**
- To avoid the possibility that only a few students participate in the connection making or that they all become an audience for your own meaning making, structure these pieces to ensure the **highest level of participation.**
- Use **active learning structures** to help students make connections.

Demonstrations

Demonstration (*n*) 1. **visual presentation** that clarifies or explains a procedure, product, or process; often illustrates a clearly articulated sequence; 2. **procedure** that gives information, provides an introduction, or shows how to do something. May prove a point about safety, form, or outcome; 3. **sequence of actions** which makes noticeable the essential steps or elements in a procedure, and indicates which steps are optional.

Tips for Giving an Effective Demonstration

♦ Classroom demonstrations occur on a regular basis, but there is little written about how to do an effective one. It appears that we are just supposed to know how to do demonstrations because we are teachers.

♦ Identify the most important points of the demonstration so that you can be sure to emphasize the critical elements. Demonstrations are more effective if you plan in advance the important points you want to demonstrate, and how you will emphasize them.

♦ Tell the students what to watch for, have them watch it, and have them **process what they saw.**

♦ Complex or lengthy demonstrations are best broken down into meaningful chunks. Allow students to process and practice between segments.

♦ **The processing of significant information is essential, because we often watch and/or notice the wrong components. Practice 10:2 Theory throughout.**

Hints

● As learners, we usually believe we can do that which we see done. But in reality, we often miss important steps. Check with your students to see if they caught what you taught.

● If students have trouble duplicating the steps you lay out in a demonstration, a **Think Aloud,** that points out potential pitfalls and common problems, might be helpful.

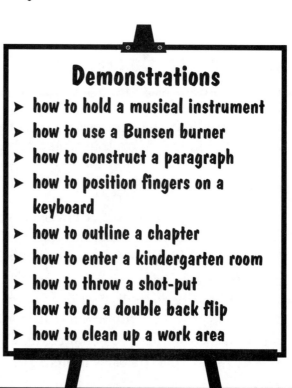

Demonstrations
- ➤ how to hold a musical instrument
- ➤ how to use a Bunsen burner
- ➤ how to construct a paragraph
- ➤ how to position fingers on a keyboard
- ➤ how to outline a chapter
- ➤ how to enter a kindergarten room
- ➤ how to throw a shot-put
- ➤ how to do a double back flip
- ➤ how to clean up a work area

An Alternative to Demonstrations...
Think Alouds

Think Aloud *(n)* an alternative to a demonstration in which the teacher assumes the role of a student "thinking aloud" about how to work through complex or confusing tasks or problems. The purpose of this format is for the teacher to point out potential pitfalls and common misconceptions or behaviors of learners, and model strategies and ways of thinking for working through the problems.

Our students think that we were born knowing how to write bibliographies and knowing all the rules of capitalization and punctuation. Why? They think so because we always seem to do it right the first time. When we do demonstrations, we show our students how a task or process is to be done; we seldom demonstrate the trial and error nature of accomplishing tasks. To help fill that void, "think alouds" were originally discussed in the reading literature (Davies, 1983) as a way to help students with reading comprehension; their use has been extended to demonstrating the perils and pitfalls of any multi-step or obscure task. (Saphier, 1990)

Process

- Identify points you want to make with a **think aloud** prior to presenting it.
- Assume the role and talk out loud about your thinking and feelings as you attempt to do the task.
- Do not interact with the audience (your students).
- Model the following as appropriate:
    - **confusion about what you are supposed to do**
    - **failure to recall all of the steps in the directions**
    - **false starts**
    - **weighing alternatives**
    - **making predictions**
    - **reviewing what you've done in similar situations**
    - **remembering what you've read or been told to do**
    - **possible frustrations**
    - **thinking of places to get help**
    - **fix-up strategies**
    - **persistence and recognition of effective efforts**
    - **feeling of success**
- When you are finished with the role play, **have students identify the strategies** you used in working through the task.
- Coach your students, or have students coach each other, in using the same process.

Simulations

A simulation is a learning experience in which students create an "as if" environment. Simulations cause learners to move into another time period, another place, or assume the perspective or role of another person. Such learning experiences move from the contrived nature of readings and worksheets and help students make personal meaning of the concepts being studied.

Simulations can be brief and spontaneous ("Pretend you have just landed at the Cairo airport") or highly structured and ongoing (a recreation of the Renaissance or a simulation of life in a rainforest). The latter requires considerable preparation and orchestration. Fortunately, there are many commercially prepared simulations available to supplement your creativity and that of your students.

Helpful Hints:

Simulations meet the needs of learners who thrive on working with others (interpersonal intelligence) and for those who need movement (kinesthetic intelligence).

Simulations provide students opportunities for cognitive and social development. Be sure to do an analysis of the plans for extensive simulations to identify the needed academic and social skills, and take action to ensure that students can be successful in the experience you are designing.

While simulations and role plays can be very powerful learning experiences, it is easy to fall into the activity completion trap (ACT) where the focus is on completion of the activity rather than on the learning outcomes. The feeling tone can go off the chart into the "fun" zone and the purpose of learning can be lost.

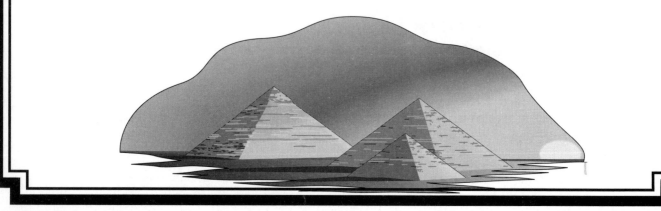

Lectures

Lecture (n) An exposition of a given subject before an audience.
Audience (n) A body of spectators, listeners, or readers of a work or performance.

Lectures are a mainstay of instructional practice. As the definitions at the top of the page indicate, the problem with lectures in isolation is that there is absolutely no guarantee of interaction between the lecturer and the audience. In *Leading the Cooperative School*, Johnson and Johnson state that one of the main problems with lectures is that **"the information passes from the notes of the professor to the notes of the students without passing through the mind of either one."** As educators, we must ensure that during a lecture the learners are purposefully interacting with the material and integrating it with their prior knowledge.

Uses of Lectures

♦ Introduce a unit

♦ Describe/present problem

♦ Share personal experiences

♦ Review most important ideas of unit

♦ Summarize a unit

♦ Provide information students cannot obtain any other way

♦ Clarify important concepts

♦ Input step in direct teaching of skills

Attributes of "Good" Lectures

♦ Address specific **objectives**

♦ Planned around a **series of questions** that the lecture answers

♦ Are **systematic, sequential**, and convey information in an **interesting** way

♦ Include **examples, stories, and analogies** that help learners relate new information to prior experiences

Lectures continued...

Potential Problems with Lectures

- ◆ Amusing anecdotes may entertain but teach little
- ◆ Lighthearted lectures may misrepresent the complexity of the material
- ◆ Incorrect or incomplete processing of content by students who mechanically write down whatever the lecturer says
- ◆ Students may be inattentive because of their roles as passive listeners and routine notetakers
- ◆ Examples, references, and stories may have little or no meaning for students or may send students off on tangents in their thinking

Lecture Enhancements

To ensure that learners do the intellectual work of "making meaning" or organizing, summarizing, and integrating the new information with prior knowledge and experiences, include one or more of the following:

- ● **Discussion Partners:** See page 59
- ● **Processing Time:** See pages 59 and 77
- ● **Written Outlines**
- ● **Graphic Organizers:** See page 229
- ● **Listening Logs**
- ● **Interactive Notebooks:** See page 227
- ● **Signal Cards:** See page 109
- ● **Accessing Prior Knowledge:** See page 53 and pages 80 -107
- ● **Checking for Understanding:** See pages 108-111

Lectures continued...
Lectures with Discussion Partners

One of the easiest ways to ensure that students are attentive and making meaning of the material being presented is to pause for processing. Since 75% of our learners are extroverted thinkers, partner discussions throughout the lecture makes a great deal of good sense.

1. Have students choose **partners** or assign partners.

2. Present for small group discussion a **focus question** or **stem** that provides a set or direction for the lecture to come (4-5 minutes).

   This discussion can focus learning, surface prior information and/or promote predictions.

   Focus questions or discussion topics can be on the board or the overhead as the students enter the area or room.

   Process in the large group as you choose. While you may want to do that on occasion to ensure accountability, you probably would not want to use the time to do it after each small group discussion or you'll never have time for your lecture!

3. Deliver the **first segment of the lecture** (10-15 minutes).

4. Give the small groups the first **processing/discussion topic** (3-4 minutes).

   Possible processing points might be for students to summarize, react to, elaborate upon, predict, resolve differences, or hypothesize answers to a question posed by the input of new information.

5. Deliver the **second segment of the lecture** (10-15 minutes).

6. Give the small groups another **processing/discussion topic** (3-4 minutes).

7. Continue **lecture segments and discussions** until the lecture is completed.

8. Give the students a **final processing focus** (5-6 minutes).

   The purpose of this closure discussion is for students to process and make connections between the bits of information presented in the lecture and hook them all onto their own "velcro."

To ensure that students are discussing what you want them to discuss, you may need to model, to circulate and listen in. Additionally, you may want to call on one or two pairs occasionally to share with the class what they have been discussing.

Adapted from *Leading the Cooperative School*, Johnson and Johnson.

Lectures continued...
Examples

Example (n) 1. one representative of a group; 2. a case or situation serving as a precedent or model for another one that is similar; 3. a problem or exercise that illustrates a method or principle.

Critical Attribute (adj, n) 1. a characteristic that is essential; 2. a quality that is basic or indispensable; 3. a component that is necessary in order for a concept to be.

Guidelines for Designing Examples to Teach Concepts & Generalizations

- Include the important characteristics and clarify what role these characteristics play in relation to the concept. We often point out or **highlight important information** about a topic **without clarifying whether these points are critical, essential, or merely interesting.**

- Help students recognize examples and non-examples of a particular thing **in isolation**. (i.e. a mixed numeral or a democracy and to be able to notice the differences **in two or more** compared concepts or objects. For example, alligator and crocodile, Celsius and Fahrenheit.)

- Use teacher or student generated examples to go beyond definitions. When teaching abstract concepts like democracy or romance we tend to rely solely on definitions. **The problem with only using definitions is that students often memorize the definition without understanding or making personal meaning of the concept.**

- When teaching **generalizations**, good examples must clearly identify the relationships and show the interaction among the **multiple concepts** contained in the generalization. **If each of the concepts is not already well understood by the students, we must explicitly teach it using their own definitions and solid examples before there is any chance that students can understand the generalization in a productive way.**

- If the concepts being taught are ones that students will use as foundations or scaffolding for other concepts, and/or if the concepts are significant enough for students to remember five years from now, we need to identify or help them to **identify and isolate the concepts' attributes.**

Lectures Examples continued...

Example (n) 1. one representative of a group; 2. a case or situation serving as a precedent or model for another one that is similar; 3. a problem or exercise that illustrates a method or principle.

Critical Attribute (adj, n) 1. a characteristic that is essential; 2. a quality that is basic or indispensable; 3. a component that is necessary in order for a concept to be.

How to Identify Critical Attributes

- List as many attributes of the concept as you can think of.
- Cross out those that are obviously not essential, but leave any that are questionable.
- Check the remaining attributes against your knowledge and other examples to ensure that the list is complete. Ask yourself if there are any examples you can think of that would meet these criteria but not be defined under the concept you are studying.
- Eliminate as many attributes as you can so that those remaining are truly essential or critical. The finished list might be only one attribute, (i.e. mammals must have mammary glands) or a set of attributes (i.e. squares must have four equal sides and four right angles).
- The remaining attributes will help differentiate the concept you are studying from other similar concepts.

Frayer Model

➤To introduce a concept
➤To help students organize what they know
➤To use while reading

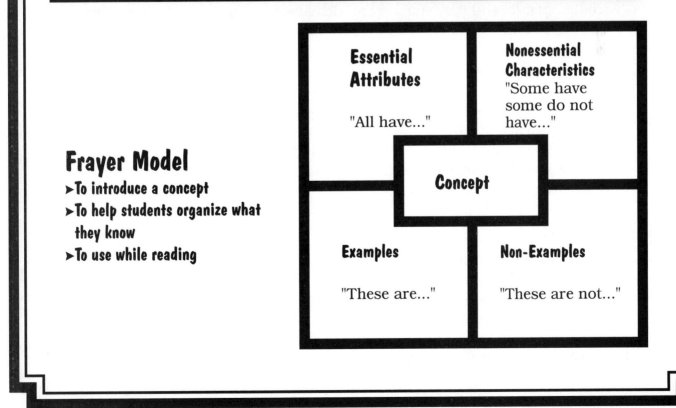

Essential Attributes

"All have..."

Nonessential Characteristics

"Some have some do not have..."

Concept

Examples

"These are..."

Non-Examples

"These are not..."

Lectures continued...
Analogies & Metaphors

Analogy (n) 1. demonstration of similarity in some respects among otherwise dissimilar things; 2. **direct analogy** is a single comparison of two objects or concepts; 3. **personal analogy** is a description of yourself as the object or concept; 4. **symbolic analogy** is a description of an object in which two words seem to be opposites or contradict each other.

Metaphor (n) a figure of speech in which a **comparison** between two unlike things is made **without** using **like** or **as**.

Simile (n) a figure of speech in which a **comparison** is made between two or more unlike things **using like** or **as**.

Purposes

♦ Analogies allow students to work from a familiar area into a new area of study. Since understanding involves connecting new learning to something already understood, analogies can be really useful for some learners. It is important to emphasize the points of comparison so that other similarities and differences do not distract from student learning.

♦ Metaphorical thinking can cause the familiar to become strange or unique as well as promote divergent thinking. If the topic is one that students have studied before, and may suffer from "delusions of familiarity," a metaphor may be just the way to re-energize their thinking around the topic.

Creating/Identifying Useful Analogies

♦ When reviewing textbooks or pieces of literature, watching television or the movies, or participating in discussions with friends and colleagues, keep the idea of building a library of useful analogies in the back of your mind.

♦ Have students create analogies and save/record the examples that have future use.

Examples

1. Paragraphs & Hamburgers

A paragraph is a group of sentences that tell about one main topic. A good paragraph is like a good hamburger. It has a fresh bun on the top (a topic sentence), a fresh bun on the bottom (a conclusion) and a lot of meat/extras in between (details & transition words).

Lectures continued...
Analogies & Metaphors

2. Bubble Gum & Muscles

What happens when you try to **blow a bubble with a fresh piece of bubble gum**? It pops, of course, or at the very best, a small bubble can be created. You have to **soften up the bubble gum** before it is pliable enough to form into large bubbles. **The same "softening up" is needed for your muscles** when you are getting ready for strenuous exercise in physical education class. It's important to "soften up" or warm up your muscles before making big movements...or you could pull a muscle and seriously injure yourself.

Powerful Possibilities

Direct Analogies

- ♦ A single comparison of two objects or concepts
- ♦ *How is the solar system like an orchestra?*

Personal Analogies

- ♦ Students develop empathy by becoming or thinking like the object or concept
- ♦ *How would you feel if you were a computer?*
  "Even though, as a computer, I am not alive, I do appear to have a mind of my own. I tell those interacting with me to, 'Please Wait.' I throw tantrums by ringing bells and flashing warning signs to those who try to force me to work faster than I can or to do a new task when I am already busy!"

Symbolic Analogies or Compressed Conflicts (a.k.a. Oxymorons)

- ♦ Description of an object in which two words seemingly are opposites or contradict each other
- ♦ *What would be an example of thundering silence?*
- ♦ *What would a slow chase look like and why might it occur?*

In addition to responding to teacher-created metaphors, students with modeling and instruction can learn to create their own.

Lectures continued...
Stories

Story (n) 1. a narrative, either true or fictitious; 2. a tale, shorter and less elaborate than a novel; 3. a narration of incidents or events; 4. archaic, to tell the history or story of.

Essential Elements of a Story

Well-told stories hold our attention because we get "to be a part of the experience" and because they make points quickly. Whether you create stories to make points or build a library of possible stories for particular points you want to make, effective stories have these elements:

➤ **a main character**

➤ **a problem or conflict**

➤ **a significant event, interaction, and/or insight that transforms or changes the main character**

➤ **a new condition, understanding, or perspective is reached.**

Variations

- ◆ short passages from literature
- ◆ quotes
- ◆ poems
- ◆ cartoons
- ◆ brief newspaper articles
- ◆ eye witness accounts
- ◆ imagery
- ◆ children's books

In the **study of a second language,** children's books in the target language are a rich source of language patterns and cultural tidbits. To find good books to use, spend an afternoon in the children's section at a library or a bookstore; the librarians or clerks in children's departments love to help!

Lord of the Flies

The Important Book

Little Red Riding Hood

The Scarlet Letter

Star Wars

Grimm's Fairy Tales

Discussions

Discussion (*n*) **1.** consideration of a question in open and usually informal debate. **2.** informal group consideration of a topic **3.** generally follows some input of information that may come from any source inside or outside the classroom.

Teacher Decisions in Planning a Discussion

1. Decide on the **purpose** of the discussion and on the mastery objectives. There may be both academic and social objectives since students will be interacting. Possible purposes are:

> **subject mastery** that includes definition of terms and identification of important concepts, application of the learning to other areas of study, and an evaluation of the author's arguments

> **issue orientation** that includes an effort to increase one's understanding of others' beliefs and feelings about the subject being studied

> **problem-solving** that requires strong background knowledge

2. Decide the **format** for the discussion. Will it be large-group/teacher-led, or small-group/student-led.

3. Consider the experience and skills of the students participating in or leading a discussion. If you are asking them to do something they have not yet demonstrated they know how to do, you may want to **"teach"** or **"model"** the **skills** you want to see.

4. Plan how long you will let the discussion continue. The objective, the importance and complexity of the issue, the product, and the discussion skills of the students will help you decide on how much **time** to allow.

5. Decide how the students will **demonstrate** what they have **learned/processed** during the discussion.

Discussions continued...

Implementation Hints:

- Communication of the **purpose** of an upcoming discussion gives students focus for reading or other data gathering.

- **Announcement** of the **outcome/product/accountability factor** in **advance** generally causes discussion groups to stay more focused.

- Start with **short sessions** on topics of **high interest** so that you can assess student skill levels for being productive in discussion groups.

- To promote more participation, have students do **brief reflective writing before the discussion begins.** That increases the likelihood that both introverted and extraverted thinkers are ready to participate.

- During discussions, teacher **circulation** from group to group listening in, clarifying as appropriate, and refocusing when necessary, is essential.

- **Process** the content, the students' responses to and questions about it, and the discussion process.

- What we call classroom discussions are often not discussions at all. They are really **recitations** during which teachers do most of the talking, calling on or giving permission to talk to certain students, asking low level questions, and tending to limit length of student answers so that more students can participate.

- Be mindful of **which students participate** in large group discussions. If many of the students are silent observers, small group discussions would foster more participation by more students.

- To more tightly **structure discussions** and ensure **equal participation,** use active learning and/or cooperative learning formats.

Attributes of a Discussion

Participants in the discussion present **multiple points of view** and are ready to change their minds after hearing convincing alternative viewpoints.

Students must **interact with each other**, as well as with the teacher.

The majority of **comments** are **longer in length** than the three or four word answers often given during a teacher led recitation.

Most of the talking is done by **students**, rather than by the teacher.

Discussion with Role Assignments...
Literature Circles

Assigned Roles and Tasks

Discussion Director

Develop a list of questions for your group to discuss. Focus on the big ideas of the reading and on sharing your reactions to the text. The best questions come from your own thoughts, feelings, and concerns.

Connector

Make connections between the readings and your life beyond this assignment. You might focus on other classes, life beyond the school day, or other readings you have studied. Record any connections you make between this reading and other parts of your life.

Passage Master

Identify the most powerful, interesting, humorous, puzzling passages in the assigned reading. During the discussion, you decide how and when to have the segments brought to the attention of the group. You may decide to read them aloud, you may ask someone else to read a segment aloud, or you may decide to have all group members read the selection silently and then discuss its significance.

Illustrator

Draw, sketch, or find a visual that captures the essence of the assigned reading or of something you thought about as you read. Use your own artistic skills, graphics, visuals from the internet, or your photo or magazine collection to identify visual images that help paint a picture about the reading. You can explain how the visual works for you, or ask group members to speculate on how the visual fits with the reading.

Essence Extractor (Summarizer)

Prepare a two to three minute summary of not only the reading, but the discussion of that reading. You may ask group members to add to the points you make via a 3-2-1 summary or a reflective journal entry.

Adapted from Harvey Daniels

A Structured Small Group Discussion...
Collaborative Controversy

Process
- Assign heterogeneous groups of four as two pairs
- Assign each pair a perspective and give students supporting materials to read
- Students present conflicting positions to one another
- Students argue strengths and weaknesses
- Students take the opposite view without reading it
- Students drop assigned roles and work as a team of four to reach consensus on the issue

Teacher promotes controversy and thinking by:
- Presenting contrasting viewpoints
- Playing devil's advocate
- Encouraging students to probe and push each other for rationale
- Monitoring how students process their actions
- Emphasizing rational and spirited discussion/argument
- Restating the question
- Asking for clarification, rationale, example, and implications. A key question is "What were the best arguments you heard from the other side?"

Sample Topics
- Line item veto
- Protecting endangered species
- Balancing the federal budget
- Expense of space exploration
- Censorship of internet
- Need for instruction in cursive handwriting
- Dress codes in schools
- Usefulness of algebra

Socratic Method of Discussion

The Socratic method is a question-and-answer method of philosophizing or discussing subjects that was used by Socrates in his early discussions with Plato. (Socrates, the teacher, would pretend to be ignorant on the subject so that Plato, the student, had to think more and become the "teacher.")

This type of discussion does not revolve around the person who is a presumed expert (the teacher).

The purpose of this discussion is for students to discover "truths," understanding, and/or new knowledge through analytical discussion with one other.

"There is only one good, knowledge,
and one evil, ignorance."
--Socrates

Socrates

- ◊ a philosopher in Athens who lived from 470 to 399 B.C.

- ◊ teacher of Plato, another great philosopher

- ◊ a stonemason by profession

- ◊ most remembered for his philosophical discussions

- ◊ led discussions with Plato and other young men who were opposed to the Athenian democratic system (Socrates himself was not one who was clearly opposed to this governmental form)

- ◊ charged with "corruption of the young"

- ◊ imprisoned, tried and sentenced to death for his association with those young anti-democrats

- ◊ died when he drank poison

Dorotha Ekx, Longmont High School, St. Vrain Valley Schools, Longmont, CO

Our Socratic Seminars

The process of preparing for and participating in a Socratic seminar is as follows:

1. Read and study a work

You will be given a work (literature, article, radio program, video, song) to read and study before the seminar. This will usually be completed as homework. Read and study it carefully. Make notes of interesting things. Also make notes of ideas or elements you don't understand.

2. Complete the Entry Ticket (E.T.)

You will be given this part of the assignment along with your reading assignment. Your reactions which you will write on your E.T. will provide you with "food for thought and discussion" and will serve as proof that you have completed your reading in a thorough and thoughtful way.

3. Participate in the seminar

You must have the entry ticket if you wish to be a part of the discussion.

The teacher will throw out the first question, which is often part of the Entry Ticket assignment.

Participants will ask questions and answer questions about the text or material you have studied.

The teacher will only intervene to remind participants to refer to the text -- "Where do you see that?" "What specific part of the story makes you feel or think that?"

As a last resort, the teacher may occasionally throw out questions to stimulate conversation, or direct the discussion toward pertinent information that has not been discovered by the participants (usually no more than one or two teacher questions per discussion).

4. If you are not participating in the seminar, you are to listen attentively and make notes of important ideas and new information.

Dorotha Ekx, Longmont High School, St. Vrain Valley Schools, Longmont, CO

Our Socratic Seminar Rules

Positive Points for...

⬧ Preparing for the seminar. Read the material; come with questions, thoughts and insights (write these down if possible).

⬧ Taking risks when reading, responding to and answering questions.

⬧ Being open-minded, compassionate and willing to change your mind.

⬧ Talking to each other, questioning each other, and listening to each other. Incite the quiet people in the class by asking them a question, or asking them to respond to what you have said.

⬧ Staying with the text. It is good to bring insight and social connection when appropriate, but remember that the goal is comprehension and insight into THIS TEXT. Point out the exact spot in the text that supports a point you are making.

⬧ Taking the time to think about a response. Try not to repeat something that has already been clearly stated by someone else.

⬧ PARTICIPATING! Everyone is needed in this exercise.

⬧ Relating a personal opinion or a belief. All opinions, emotions and concerns are valid (as long as they relate to the text in some way).

⬧ Speaking clearly and loudly as you make eye contact with all of the participants.

⬧ Learning as much as you can from others. It is O.K. to take notes. In fact, you may want to record some information that you will use later in an essay or on a test.

⬧ Asking your peers questions that will help you to understand the material. If you don't understand the story or the text, that is no excuse for not participating! You will only lose points when you do not try to be involved in the discussion.

Negative points for...

⬧ Not participating.
⬧ Not paying attention or doing other work when in the audience or in the seminar group.
⬧ Carrying on side conversations while in the audience or in the seminar group.
⬧ Being a distraction in any way to those who are participating in the discussion.

Dorotha Ekx, Longmont High School, St. Vrain Valley Schools, Longmont, CO

Active Learning

Tell me,
I forget.

Show me,
I remember.

Involve me,
I understand.

- Ancient Chinese Proverb

IV

Active Learning

TOP TEN QUESTIONS
to ask myself as I design lessons

1. What should **students know and be able to do** with what they know as a result of this lesson? How are these objectives related to national, state, and/or district standards or proficiencies?

2. How will **students demonstrate what they know and what they can do** with what they know? What will be the **assessment criteria**, and what form will it take?

3. How will I find out what students already know, and how will I help them access what they know and have experienced both inside and outside the classroom? How will I help them not only build on prior experiences but deal with their misconceptions and reframe their thinking when appropriate?

4. How will new knowledge, concepts, and skills be introduced? Given the diversity of my students, what are **my best options for sources and presentation modes** of new material?

5. How will I facilitate student processing (meaning making) of new information or processes? What are the key questions, activities, and assignments (in class or homework)?

6. How will I check for student understanding during the lesson?

7. What do I need to do to **differentiate instruction** so that the learning experiences are productive for all students?

8. How will I **"Frame the Learning"** so that **students know the objectives**, the **rationale** for the objectives and activities, the directions and procedures, as well as the **assessment criteria** at the beginning of the learning process?

9. How will I build in opportunities for students to make real world connections and to learn and use the varied and complex thinking skills they need to succeed in the classroom and the world beyond?

10. What adjustments need to be made in the **learning environment** so that we can work and learn efficiently during this study?

Active Learning

Self Assessment:
These statements describe the learning environment...
Almost always (A), Sometimes (S), Never (N)

___ **1.** I encourage students to express varied opinions as long as they support those opinions with data.

___ **2.** I encourage students to think about how the information they are learning relates to other subjects and their lives beyond the school day.

___ **3.** My students think critically and creatively because I ask questions that have more than one answer.

___ **4.** I encourage students to think and discuss answers with a partner or a small group before answering in the larger group.

___ **5.** I encourage my students to reflect on their experiences when learning something new and they often "mess with" new ideas before lectures or reading.

___ **6.** I help students examine their own thinking and build on their ideas.

___ **7.** I ask students what they already know about a unit before introducing it.

___ **8.** I use essential questions and key concepts to help students organize new information in ways that make sense to them.

___ **9.** Students share responsibility for generating their own vocabulary lists and the questions they want answered.

___ **10.** Students resolve their differences by discussing their thinking.

___ **11.** Class time spent on practice exercises & learning the facts leads to meaningful use of the skills and facts in the near future.

___ **12.** I encourage students to try solving difficult problems, even before they learn all the material.

___ **13.** Students are allowed to explore topics that excite or interest them.

___ **14.** I design assessments around real world applications.

___ **15.** Students help determine how they demonstrate learning and how they are assessed.

Adapted from *The Student Constructivism and Active Learning Environments Scale* (The S.C.A.L.E.) by Bonk & Medury, 1991

I Forgot!

Ebbinghaus

When Hermann Ebbinghaus, a German psychologist, investigated memory using nonsense syllables, he found that **forgetting sets in very quickly**. Amazingly, of all that is forgotten during the first month after learning. **47 percent of forgetting occurs in the first twenty minutes** with 62 percent occurring within the first day. This research from the nineteenth century clearly indicates that the **prime time to process, discuss, and reflect is immediately after new information is presented (either in class or in independent study), before forgetting sets in.** This explains why we have problems deciphering notes we take during a lecture or presentation if we do not apply the information immediately.

Hermann Ebbinghaus, *Memory.* Columbia University Press, 1913. First published in German in 1885.

H. F. Spitzer

In the 1930s, H. F. Spitzer analyzed the forgetting patterns of more than 3,000 students. Spitzer, in this study that used textbook material, discovered that:

1. The greatest amount of forgetting occurs rapidly, during the first day after material is presented. (This matches the findings of Ebbinghaus in the previous century.)
2. Forgetting continues a quick pace for the first two weeks.
3. **Forgetting slows down after two weeks**, but then again, **there is not much left to forget.**

H. F.. Spitzer, "Studies in Retention," *Journal of Educational Psychology*, 1939, p. 641-656.

Rate of Forgetting Textbook Material

After one day, 46% forgotten
After seven days, 65% forgotten
After fourteen days, 79% forgotten
After twenty-one days, 82% forgotten

10:2 Theory

Learners make sense of new information by integrating it with prior knowledge. During lectures or other presentations of new information, they take mental breaks to accomplish this task. Learners take these breaks even as more information is being presented. **Mary Budd Rowe** (1983) recommends that we provide short processing pauses at regularly scheduled intervals to accommodate these mental lapses.

Mental lapses occur when . . .

- **short term memory overloads** because too many new ideas are introduced in a given period . . . meanwhile, the discussion or lecture flows on!

- **an idea is not immediately grasped.** There is momentary confusion while a student tries to "make sense" of the information. If a suitable long-term "file" exists for the student, the transfer to long term memory occurs quickly. If, however, files have to be created or reorganized, the transfer takes longer . . . meanwhile, the discussion or lecture flows on!

- **different words or symbols are used by different sources** to identify the same chunk of knowledge. For example, a teacher might refer to a concept in one set of terms, a parent in another. The learner needs time to sort for similarities, differences, and patterns . . . meanwhile, the discussion or lecture flows on!

- **students are sent off on a mental detour** by something they hear in the discussion or lecture. This occurs when students are well versed in the content material. Even if the mental detour is an important mental exercise, they miss the content presented . . . meanwhile, the discussion or lecture flows on!

To reduce the information loss, Rowe recommends that we pause for two minutes at about ten minute intervals . . . hence the name, 10:2 Theory. For every ten minutes or so of meaningful chunks of new information, learners should be provided with two or so minutes to process information. Small groups share notes and/or discuss their current understanding and memory to fill in or supplement gaps.

When you and your students are just getting started with collaborative and small group work, remember...

IT'S HARD to GET LEFT OUT of a PAIR

Think BIG

Start small!

See **LEARNING BUDDIES** and **THINK-PAIR-SHARE** for two great starting points for having students work in pairs.

Active Learning Structures

- ❖ Corners
- ❖ Frame of Reference
- ❖ Graffiti
- ❖ Inside-Outside Circles
- ❖ Kinetic Cards (5)
- ❖ Learning Buddies
- ❖ Line-Ups
- ❖ Numbered Heads Together
- ❖ Scavenger Hunt
- ❖ Stir the Class
- ❖ Take A Stand (5)
- ❖ Think-Pair-Share
- ❖ Three Column Charts
- ❖ Walking Tour

Corners

Process

- Pose a question that has multiple answers or asks students to rank order several options.

- Give students time to consider their own thinking about the topic, then have them move to a corner of the room that has been designated as the meeting place of all those holding the same opinion or view.

- In the corner meeting places, have students discuss why they think or believe the way they do. If the groups are large, have students divide into pairs or triads so that all can voice their opinions and their rationales.

- As appropriate, have selected students or volunteers report for their corner. Large group sharing can be oral only or the corner groups can also generate and share charts listing their rationales for choosing that particular answer/viewpoint.

Sample Topics

- ◆ CEOs of major corporations salaries should be....give alternative amounts, ratios, rationales for setting salaries.
- ◆ Which professions are most in demand now?
- ◆ Which character in the book would you most like to meet?
- ◆ What volleyball skill would you most like to develop?
- ◆ If you were the leader of your country/state, which issue would be your top priority...A, B, C, or D?
- ◆ How strongly do you agree or disagree with the statement, "All forms of violence should be censored on television"?
- ◆ Predict the percentage of people who will respond affirmatively to stated survey questions.
- ◆ Name four inventions; which is most significant and why?
- ◆ Name four historical figures; who changed the world the most and why?

Frame of Reference

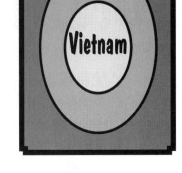

Purpose

These initial notations help students surface prior knowledge or related experiences and are also helpful to the teacher in understanding where students are coming from as they enter the study of new material.

Process

- The **topic or issue** to be discussed is placed in the center of the matted frame where a picture would be placed in a picture frame.

- Students are given several minutes to individually jot down **words or phrases** that come to mind when they hear or see the term "pictured." These words go in the "mat" area of their frame of reference.

- Students are then asked to jot down how they came to know what they know or think...that is the sources, people, events that have **influenced their thinking**. These reactions go in the "frame" area of the graphic.

- Following the individual reflection and writing, students are asked to share their "frames of reference" with a partner or a small group.

Variations

A variation of **Frame of Reference** can be used to process learning by having students place the name of a historical character in the center. The students then jot down how this person would describe his or her own life and times and then the events and people who influenced his or her thinking. Assigning different students different persons/perspectives can lead to powerful "in the voice of" discussions when the historical frames of references are completed.

Frame of Reference can also be used as an introductory and community building exercise. Students put their own names in the center, describe themselves and then cite those people and events that have shaped their thinking and lives.

Graffiti

Saphier and Haley call this strategy Carousel Brainstorming.

Process

- Write problems, formulas, sentences to be translated, or ideas to brainstorm on pieces of large chart paper and post around the room. Students move in small groups from chart to chart.

    or

- Give each piece of chart paper to a group of three or four. Students work at their tables and the charts move from table to table. Kathy Anderson of New Trier High School, Winnetka, Illinois calls this version **Ready...Rotate**.

    In either case,

- each group works on a different question, topic, issue, or statement related to the concept being studied and writes responses or "graffiti" which can be short words, phrases, or graphics on their chart paper.

- After the alloted time period, have the students or the charts move.

- Repeat the process until all groups have reacted to all charts.

- Post the charts and have students react to the statements or topics, identify patterns, and/or make predictions based on what is written/drawn on the charts.

Variations

- This strategy can be used any time during a lesson or unit. At the beginning you and your students can find out what they already know and can do; in the middle it is a useful way for you and them to check on their learning. At the end of study, it can serve as a great review for an exam or even for predicting what might be on the exam.

- Individuals or groups can use different color markers to track contributions.

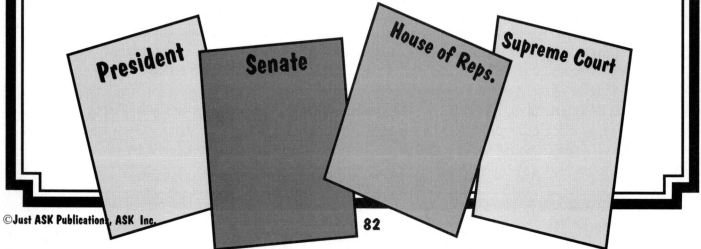

Inside-Outside Circles

Process

- On index cards, **write vocabulary words, math or science problems, or questions** about important points in the unit. Give a card to each student. Have students turn the cards over and **write the answer to their question on the back of the card.**

- Have the students number/letter off as "1s" and "2s" or "As" and "Bs". Ask one subset to stand and form a circle. When the circle is formed, have them face the outside of the circle. The other students then go and stand facing a student in the "inside" circle.

- **Have students ask each other their questions.** Advise them, if their partner does not know the answer, to immediately show them the question and the answer.

  - **As ask their questions of the Bs.**

  - **Bs then ask their questions of the As.**

  - **At the signal, students switch cards. Now the As have the Bs cards and vice versa.**

- Have the outside circle move to the left or the right until they reach the second or third person in the inside circle.

- These new partners quiz each other as before. Continue this sequence for as long as is appropriate.

- It is important to have the students **exchange cards** or they will get bored asking the same question over and over and won't learn nearly as much.

Variation on a theme...
Cake Walk

- Questions are written on the board or on an overhead transparency.

- Students form concentric circles.

- The teacher or a student plays music. While the music plays, the circles move in opposite directions. When the music stops, students in the outer circle turn to face students in the inner circle.

- Students discuss the question to which their attention is directed.

- Repeat the process for as long as it is appropriate.

Adapted from Spencer Kagan

Kinetic Cards

Kinesthetic learners need to "handle the information." The "card activities" on pages 84-88 offer opportunities for "hands on learning." Index cards, post-it notes, or the backs of old handouts cut into 4" x 6" segments will work equally well.

Sort Cards

Process

1. Students, working individually, generate words and short phrases that come to mind when they think of a designated topic. They record each idea on a separate index card.

2. Working in small groups, students:
   - share ideas
   - clarify similar ideas
   - eliminate duplicates

3. Students sort the ideas of the group into categories. The categories can be created by the students or the teacher can identify categories for student use.

4. When the sorting and labeling is completed, the students take a tour around the room to observe and analyze the work of other groups. One student stays behind at the base table to answer questions.

5. Groups return to tables to discuss what they observed and to revise or add new ideas/categories.

6. Groups use the generated ideas and categories as a basis of future study or discussion.

7. Ask students to do meta-cognitive processing; that is, have them process how they went about their thinking as they generated, sorted, categorized, labeled, and analyzed the work of others.

Sort Cards
5 Card Draw
All Hands on Deck
Tic-Tac-Toe
I Have the Question, Who Has the Answer?

I Have the Question,
Who Has the Answer?

Purposes
- Review concepts through active student participation
- Heighten attention and engagement of all students

Materials
- **Two sets of index cards**, or slips of paper, old worksheets cut up. One set contains questions related to the unit of study. The second set contains the answers to the questions. **Hint: To keep students engaged, prepare more answer cards than question cards.**

Process
- Distribute **answer cards** to students.
- Place a stack of **question cards** face down in the middle of each of the student tables.
- Designate a student to turn over a question card. The student says **"The Question is...Who has the answer?"**
- All students check their answer cards to see if they have the correct answer or a possible one. If a student thinks he/she has an answer, she reads the answer. If it is a match, the student with the answer turns over the next question card, reads the question aloud, and the process continues.

Variations
- The whole group owns the answers distributed to individuals and they collaborate in deciding if they have a good answer.
- Start with just a few questions and answers for students and add to the collection as the unit progresses.
- Have students prepare the cards.
- Use the question/answer cards for individual/small group review.

All Hands on Deck

Purposes
- To promote participation by all students in a brainstorming process
- To focus students on topic/concept to be studied
- To find out what students know about the topic to be studied

Process
- Post chart paper listing subsets of the concept/unit to be studied around the room.
- Give examples of ideas that might be included in each category or on each chart.
- Provide each **group of students** with a **stack of index cards** with the same topic headings as found on the posted chart paper.
- **Each student takes one or two cards** (exact number determined by the number of students in each group and the number of subsets).
  - Each student has 60 to 90 seconds to brainstorm ideas about the subsets on their cards, with the expectation that each student will contribute at least one idea to each card.
  - When given the signal, cards are passed to the left and the next student adds ideas to the subset card just received. **Cards circulate** within the group until each student has written on each card.
  - A team reporter reads one contribution from their team for the selected chart on the wall in round-robin fashion. When one chart is completed, focus moves to the next chart.

Variation
Provide groups with sheets of paper with topics printed at the top and small **post-it notes.** Students write their ideas on the notes and stick them to paper. Large group sharing can be through **posting of the notes** and a **walking tour** of the charts. Each student in the small groups could be given a different color post-it note to further hold each student accountable for participation.

Card Categories...
Five Card Draw

Purposes

- place students in working groups
- review/preview content specific
- practice categorizing skills

Process

♦ Prepare cards with vocabulary words, geographic locations, components of mathematical equations or formulas, or items from any set of categories. To fit the name, **"Five Card Draw,"** identify **five items/cards for each set** and prepare the number of sets you need to have one card per student.

♦ As students enter the room, have them draw a card or have them draw (from a deck) as you circulate around the room.

♦ Students are to move around the room to find four other students who "fit" with the category represented by the item on the card.

♦ Once the groups have formed, students sit together and study/review material and categories represented by their cards. They are expected to figure out exactly how they fit together and prepare to present/explain their material to the class. Each member should be able to define, explain, or demonstrate all the concepts the group represents.

♦ The discussion and/or review can continue using one of several formats. To continue the random selection format, you could have students number off at each table, then spin a spinner or draw a straw, and have the selected student answer a question related to the material being studied.

♦ Other students could have listening logs, learning logs, or journals in which they are recording the information presented.

Tic-Tac-Toe

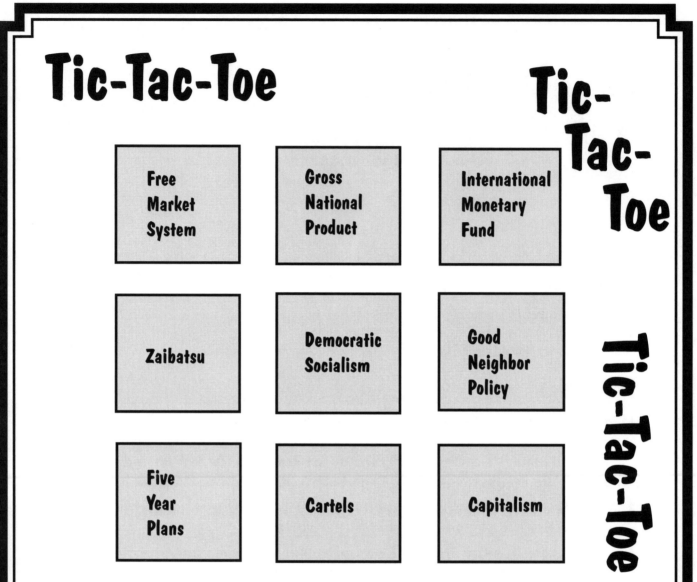

Free Market System	Gross National Product	International Monetary Fund
Zaibatsu	Democratic Socialism	Good Neighbor Policy
Five Year Plans	Cartels	Capitalism

Purpose

To have students go beyond memorizing definitions and to look for patterns and **connections** embedded in the vocabulary words and concepts being studied.

Process

- Place, or have students place, vocabulary words or important concepts on **index cards.**
- Give each student or group a set of cards.
- Have students shuffle their cards and deal out nine cards in a **3x3 format.**
- Ask students to form eight sentences each, including the three words straight across in a **row**, straight down in a **column**, or on the **diagonals.**
- Have the students or groups share the sentences that capture important **connections**, or "misconnections," between words and concepts being studied.

Learning Buddies or Partners

Process

♦ Students can self-select another student with whom to do **10:2 processing** or with whom to do **Think-Pair-Share.**

♦ The teacher announces a processing time. A focus question or process direction is given to define the task for the partners.

♦ To build in movement, have the partners stand together as they follow the teacher's directions or answer the question. The time for these processing discussions is generally brief; 2-4 minutes is the norm.

♦ Teacher circulation and listening in on the discussions provides a great deal of information about what the students are learning and/or are puzzled about. It also helps hold the students accountable for talking about the designated topic.

Variations

♦ Pairs can be carefully crafted by the teacher or randomly partnered by pulling names out of the hat, matching cards, counting off, etc.

♦ **Clock Buddies, Element Buddies, Parent Function Partners,** etc. are efficient, long term, content specific adaptations of this structure. Students are given a graphic with slots for ten to twelve "appointments." At each slot, two students record each other's name. This sign-up period takes about four to five minutes and provides an efficient way for students to interact during the next few weeks. Whenever the teacher announces a time for students to process learning, a partnership is identified and students meet with their partner.

Clock Buddies

Elements Buddies

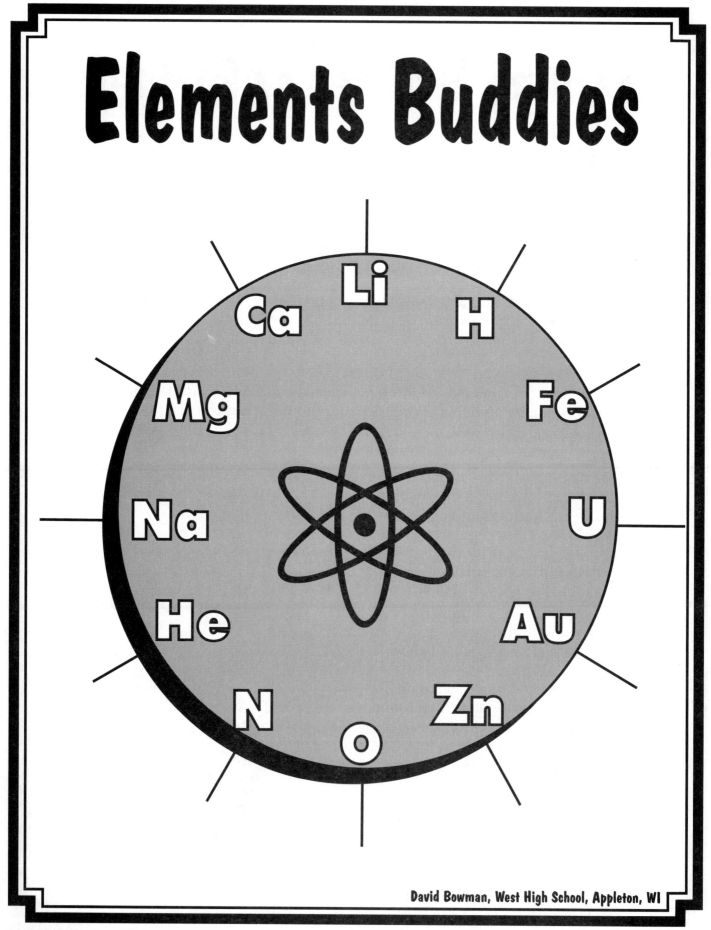

David Bowman, West High School, Appleton, WI

Parent Function Partners

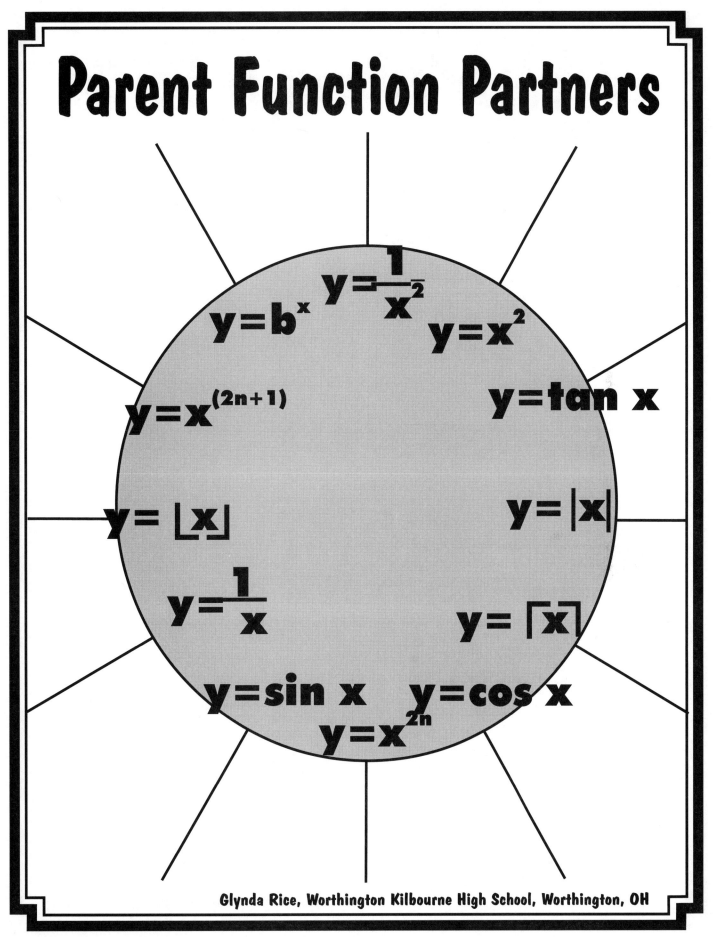

$$y = \frac{1}{x^2}$$
$$y = b^x$$
$$y = x^2$$
$$y = x^{(2n+1)}$$
$$y = \tan x$$
$$y = \lfloor x \rfloor$$
$$y = |x|$$
$$y = \frac{1}{x}$$
$$y = \lceil x \rceil$$
$$y = \sin x \quad y = \cos x$$
$$y = x^{2n}$$

Glynda Rice, Worthington Kilbourne High School, Worthington, OH

South America Learning Buddies

Mike Rutherford, Manassas City Schools, Manassas, VA

Line-Ups

Purposes

- To get students to take and defend a position on a topic
- To evoke curiosity and heighten attention/focus during instruction
- To help students fine tune their estimation skills
- To help students develop their ability to articulate their rationale

Process

1. Have students **take a stand, make a prediction, or make an estimation** pertaining to the topic of instruction. Have them write their predictions on a small piece of paper or a post-it note.

2. Designate one end of the room as the low end/beginning and the other as the high end/ending. Have students **line up in the order** of their predictions or estimates. Have students hold their written estimate where it can be seen and line up without talking.

3. Have students **report their estimates** so that all students can see the wide range of responses

4. **Fold the line** on itself so the person with the highest estimate or the end is facing the person with the lowest response. Or, find the center of the line and have the students move so that the person holding the highest estimate is facing someone with a mid-level response.

5. The partners **share their estimates as well as the rationales and strategies** they used to determine their responses. Students can be asked to report on their partner's answers and rationale or on their own.

6. If there is a correct answer, you may want to have them determine it or do research to find out the **answer** or the **opinions of experts** in the field.

Examples

- **Sequence the steps in changing a tire. Place one step on each slip of paper and distribute randomly.**
- **How many hours of television do most 18 year-olds watch in one week?**
- **How much is spent on the marketing of a best-selling book?**
- **What is the life expectancy of the average female in the United States?**
- **Estimate the percentage of Americans (French) who exercise the right to vote.**

Spencer Kagan, 1990

Metric Line-Up

You have received a card bearing the name (or abbreviation) of a unit of measure. When given the signal, you will have 2 minutes to **sort yourselves into 2 groups (either MASS or LENGTH). Then you must line up in order from largest to smallest unit.** (If both the name and the abbreviation are present, those two individuals should be side by side.) No talking!

After I have checked your group, list the units in order (abbreviations are okay). For each unit having a prefix, write 2 equivalencies in the form shown below:

ex: $1 \text{ kg} = 10^{?}\text{g}$ & $1 \text{ g} = 10^{?}$

Unit	Equivalence #1	Equivalence #2

Gillian Thomsen, New Trier High School, Winnetka, IL

Numbered Heads Together

Process

- Have students form teams of 4 or 5.
- Have students within each team count off from 1-4 or 5 (depending on the number of group members). If teams are uneven, when #5 is called to answer, the #4 person on 4 member teams answers with the #5 people from 5 member teams.
- The teacher asks a question.
- **Students put their heads together** and collaboratively generate an answer.
- Members of the team make sure each member can answer the question.
- The teacher calls a number at random. All students assigned that number stand or raise their hands; one of these students is selected to answer the question.

Variations

- Using a spinning wheel, dice, or playing cards to identify the spokesperson makes this structure even more engaging.
- If the answer has several parts, #1 from one table can answer the first part, than another #1 adds the second part, etc.
- When a student gives a partially correct answer, another person with that number can be called upon to add to the response. Another variation is to have all teams put their heads together again to check understanding and supply the missing information.
- When divergent answers are the goal, use **Numbered Head Ambassadors** to have the identified group member move to the next table to tell that group what the ambassador's "home" group thinks.

Russ Barr, Chaparral Middle School, Diamond Bar, CA

Canada Scavenger Hunt

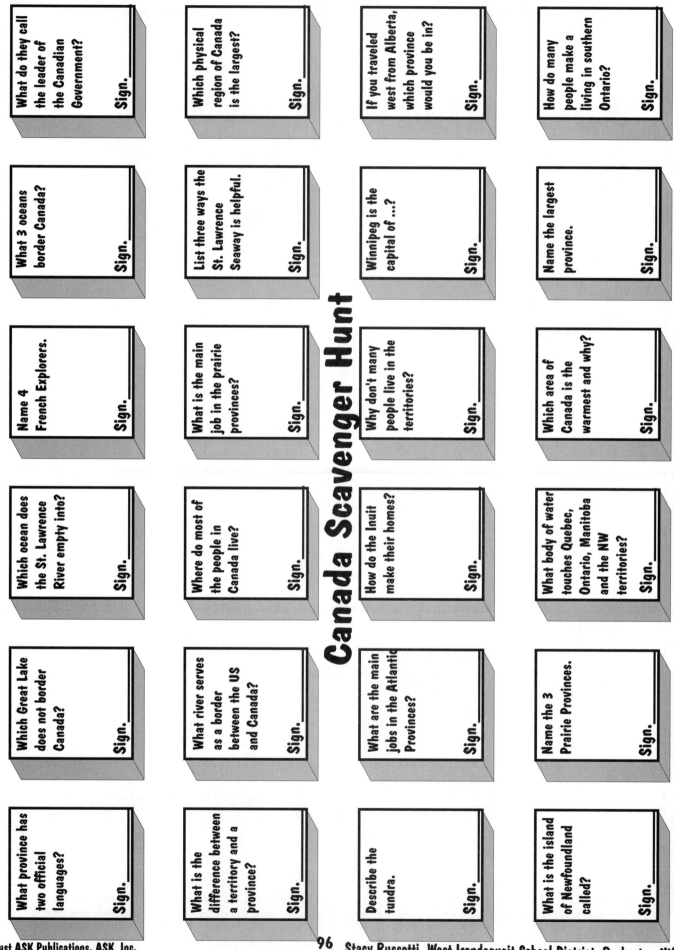

What do they call the leader of the Canadian Government?

Sign. _____

Which physical region of Canada is the largest?

Sign. _____

If you traveled west from Alberta, which province would you be in?

Sign. _____

How do many people make a living in southern Ontario?

Sign. _____

What 3 oceans border Canada?

Sign. _____

List three ways the St. Lawrence Seaway is helpful.

Sign. _____

Winnipeg is the capital of …?

Sign. _____

Name the largest province.

Sign. _____

Name 4 French Explorers.

Sign. _____

What is the main job in the prairie provinces?

Sign. _____

Why don't many people live in the territories?

Sign. _____

Which area of Canada is the warmest and why?

Sign. _____

Which ocean does the St. Lawrence River empty into?

Sign. _____

Where do most of the people in Canada live?

Sign. _____

How do the Inuit make their homes?

Sign. _____

What body of water touches Quebec, Ontario, Manitoba and the NW territories?

Sign. _____

Which Great Lake does not border Canada?

Sign. _____

What river serves as a border between the US and Canada?

Sign. _____

What are the main jobs in the Atlantic Provinces?

Sign. _____

Name the 3 Prairie Provinces.

Sign. _____

What province has two official languages?

Sign. _____

What is the difference between a territory and a province?

Sign. _____

Describe the tundra.

Sign. _____

What is the island of Newfoundland called?

Sign. _____

Stacy Russotti, West Irondequoit School District, Rochester, NY

Scavenger Hunt

Purposes

- To review, preview, and expand a topic.
- To demonstrate to students that collectively they know a great deal.

Process

- Prepare a set of questions on a topic.

- If students are not already in table groups or teams, they will need groups to discuss their work after the scavenger hunt.

- **Have students individually read** through the questions, **select one** on which they will be the expert, and **answer only that one** on their sheets. As an alternative, you may assign a specific question to each student or have them draw the question number out of a hat.

- You may wish to initial the answers before they start the hunt to ensure that a "virus" does not spread around the room, or you may wish to let students discover and deal with any errors.

- Students can use **all the people and materials** in the room as resources to obtain the rest of the answers. Students may only obtain one answer from each person they ask.

- **Answers can "flow through"** one person to another, but the "third party" and middle person should be prepared to fully explain the answer. The name the student lists as a resource is the person from whom they actually obtain the answer.

- When time is called, students return to their table groups or teams, verify answers, and complete any unfinished answers.

- Only unresolved issues need be discussed with the entire class.

Stir the Class

Process

- Provide each student with a data collection sheet containing ten to twenty lines, or have them number their own sheets.

- Have each student write, as directed, three reasons, three causes, three points of interest, etc., about the topic/concept to be studied. Ask them to make the third one on their list unique.

- At a signal, students move around the room collecting/giving one idea from/to each student. Ideas received from one student can be passed "through" to another student.

- After an appropriate amount of time, students return to their seats. At this point, you can have students compare lists, prioritize, categorize, design research projects, etc.

- At this point, students can continue with a lesson format appropriate to the level of thinking you want them to do. They have had time to focus on the subject and to hear ideas from classmates.

Possible Topics

- Ways we use **AVERAGES** in daily life...
- Potential problems with a **FLAT INCOME TAX**..
- Significant pieces of **LITERATURE** you've read..
- Animals that live in **AFRICA**...
- Causes of **PREJUDICE**...
- Places you see or use **METRIC MEASUREMENT**...
- Primary causes of **EROSION**...
- Facts about **INUITS**...
- Effects of human behavior on the **ECOSYSTEM**...
- **HEROES, HEROINES, EXTRAORDINARY LEADERS, VILLAINS, GREEK GODS, COMMUNITY HELPERS**, etc.
- Spanish words related to **TRAVEL**...

TAKE A STAND

Purposes

- To motivate students through controversy
- To give students a purpose for reading
- To use students' experience base to involve them in new learning

Process

- Identify the **main points** students are to grapple with in a reading, video, or other source.

- Create five to ten **statements** related to those points. Some of the statements should be true and others false. Display the statements on an overhead, chart, or individual handouts.

- When each statement is read, either by the students or the teacher, the students record their responses on their statement sheet or use another means to express their **opinion.** Pam Lecy of Appleton, Wisconsin uses signal cards with **"AGREE"** on one side and **"DISAGREE"** on the other.

- After students have taken a stand on the statements, but before they read the material, discuss the pros and cons of each statement so that students hear **rationales** for varying positions.

- Students then consult the information source. As they work, students record information or note location of information that **refers to, supports, or contradicts** the position.

- The lesson can be continued in a variety of ways. In follow-up **discussion**, students can talk about what surprised them, what they learned, and continue to cite other sources of information that presents different perspectives.

Variations...See the next four pages for directions.

- ◆ **Exclusion Brainstorming**
- ◆ **Facts and Folklore**
- ◆ **Anticipation Guide**
- ◆ **Personal Opinion Guide**

Take a Stand...
Exclusion Brainstorming

Purposes
- To predict and set a focus for learning
- To find out what students think they know about a topic
- To build skills for analyzing possible connections

Process
- Write a topic on the chalkboard. Under the topic, write a series of words, including:

   some words that clearly fit the topic

   others that clearly do not fit the topic

   and others that are ambiguous
- Students identify which words they think fit the topic by drawing a line through those that are not related and drawing a circle around those they think are related.
- Students then explain or discuss why they chose the way they did.
- Students then explore the topic by reading, viewing, or visiting.
- Students compare their predictions to their findings.

Hints
- This method is especially productive if the group is small or not yet skilled in the brainstorming process, because the teacher does the list-making and students systematically build skills.
- Students may learn to develop these lists for their classmates to respond to. This learning experience would be a good one as an extension and enrichment activity.

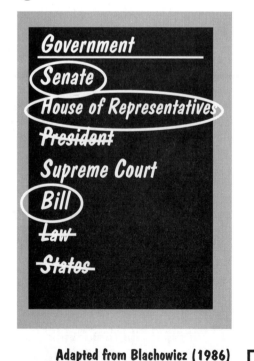

Adapted from Blachowicz (1986)

Take a Stand...
Facts & Folklore

Purposes

- To discover what students "know"...correctly and incorrectly...about a topic
- To differentiate between truth and fiction for concepts with much information in both forms
- To validate the existence of folklore

Process

- Have students list all they know about a topic. Encourage them to list "folklore" as well as "facts." This can be done individually, in small groups, or in large groups.
- Have them identify which ideas they think are fact and which they think are opinion or fantasy.
- Discuss with the students why they made their choices.

Examples

- **Facts and Folklore** is useful when beginning a topic widely covered in the media, such as a court case or a sport star, to help students learn to separate "hype" from "fact".
- Try **Facts and Folklore** when beginning a unit on a foreign country to see what the students' preconceptions are. For example, on the topic of "The Middle East", students might respond: "They make a lot of oil," "The women have to stay inside all the time," "They speak another language," "Hussein lives there." When students share their ideas, you can learn which topics you will need to clarify as you teach.

Possibilities

- George Washington
- Substance Abuse
- Difference in Cultures
- Columbus
- Dinosaurs
- Metric System

Take a Stand...
Anticipation Reaction Guide

An example of the Anticipation/Reaction Guide developed by Bean and Peterson.

Directions:

1.   Respond to each statement **before** you read.   **T=true**   **F=false**

2.   Read section B.9, page 11.5

3.   Respond to each statement **after** you read.   **T=true**   **F=false**

4.   Rewrite the statements that are false so that they are true.

Before Reading   **After Reading**

_____1.   Many properties of elements are determined   _____
            largely by the number of protons in their
            atoms and how these protons are arranged.

_____2.   Metal atoms lose their outer electrons more   _____
            easily than do nonmetal atoms.

_____3.   Active metals can give up one or more of   _____
            their electrons to ions of less-active metals.

_____4.   Stronger attractions among atoms of a metal   _____
            result in higher boiling points.

_____5.   Understanding the properties of atoms does   _____
            not help to predict and correlate the behavior
            of materials.

Cholesterol

Lynn Hiller, New Trier High School, Winnetka, IL

Take a Stand...
Personal Opinion Guide

for

The Scarlet Ibis by James Hurst

Before You Read: Work with a partner on this exercise. Read each statement below and put a + (plus) mark in the space under the Before Reading column if you agree with the statement, or put a - (minus) sign if you disagree with the statement. Use your personal experience, knowledge, and opinions to make your decision. After you have completed all statements, take turns with your partner and read each again. Explain why you agree or disagree with each other.

Before Reading   ## After Reading

_____	**1.** Pride is a wonderful thing.	_____
_____	**2.** Pride is a terrible thing.	_____
_____	**3.** Children can be cruel.	_____
_____	**4.** It's possible to like and dislike a person at the same time.	_____
_____	**5.** We should always be proud of our families.	_____
_____	**6.** Sometimes family members can be embarrassing.	_____
_____	**7.** A good deed is only worth doing if you get recognition for doing it.	_____
_____	**8.** Brothers and/or sisters are nothing but trouble.	_____
_____	**9.** It's uncomfortable to be around a handicapped person.	_____
_____	**10.** Feeling guilty is an awful burden.	_____

Read the piece of literature. Look for issues in the story that are relevant to these statements.

After You Read: Re-read the statement and mark your responses in the After Reading column. Tomorrow in class, you and your partner will compare your reactions and discuss your selections based on your interpretation of the story.

Mickie Froehlich, New Trier High School, Winnetka, IL

Think-Pair-Share

Process

- Ask a question.
- Ask students to think quietly about possible answers to the question; this is usually only thirty seconds to one minute, unless the question is quite complex. **(THINK)**
- Have students pair with a neighbor or a learning buddy to discuss their thinking. The discussion usually lasts two to three minutes. **(PAIR)**
- Ask students to share their responses with the whole group or with a table group. Not all students have to share their answers with the large group. **(SHARE)**

Some teachers use hand signals, pointers, bells, cubes, etc. to mark transition points during the cycle. When appropriate, students can write notes, web or diagram their responses during the "Think" or "Pair" time. Students can either explain their own thinking, that of their partners or the consensus they reached. Think-Pair-Share can be used 2-5 times during an instructional period.

Benefits to Students

- provides the processing time called for in 10:2 theory
- builds in wait time
- provides rehearsal
- enhances depth and breadth of thinking

- increases level of participation

Benefits to the Teacher

- provides opportunities to check for understanding
- provides time for teacher to make instructional decisions
- provides time for teacher to locate support materials and plan the next question
- allows the teacher to intervene with one or two students without an audience.

Frank Lyman is often credited with inventing this strategy which has become a widely disseminated part of our practice.

Three Column Charts

Purposes

- To help students access prior knowledge through brainstorming
- To identify areas of student interest or concern
- To aid the teacher in planning lessons as well as checking for understanding
- To track student learning throughout unit
- To identify areas for further student research/study

Process

- Use this strategy prior to, during, or at the close of any unit of study. The process can be done individually, in small groups, or as a class activity.
- Announce topic and column titles; post on charts or have students record in table groups.
- Have the teacher or students record student responses to the stems. The student who offers the idea tells the recorder which column to put it in.
- During the brainstorming phase, emphasize getting lots of ideas rather than debating or discussing the ideas as they are generated. Debates, clarifications, and discussion of ideas occur once the brainstorming is over. The teacher does not clarify any confusions or react in any way other than to record the data. Conflicting data may be recorded.
- During the lesson or unit of study points of misconception, confusion, or curiosity are addressed.

Choose any one of the following sets of column headings or create your own.

What I Knew	What I Now Know	What I Still Don't Know
What I know...	What I don't know...	What I wish I knew...
Productive...	Somewhat productive...	Unproductive...
Most important....	Somewhat important...	Not important at all...
Already know...	Want to know...	Learned...
In reading vocab...can read, use in writing & use in discussion...	In reading vocab...can read, but don't use it...	Never heard/saw it before...

Walking Tour

Purposes

- To introduce complex texts, provocative ideas, or discrepancies
- To emphasize key ideas of content material
- To raise curiosity and increase speculation about a subject

Process

- **Compose five to eight charts** that represent the content material, pictorially or verbally. Use photographs of places or objects, direct quotes from the text, or other means to convey one idea per chart. For example, for a study of France, charts might contain postcards, phrases in French, and/or a map of France. *Hint*: **If the tour is used to introduce complex concepts or a complex reading, isolate the primary points and create one chart for each point.**

- **Post the charts** around the classroom and number each chart. Divide students into "touring groups" to fit the classroom space, age of students, and complexity of the material.

- **Assign one group per chart** as a starting point. Groups spend two to five minutes at that chart, taking notes on, and/or discussing the idea presented.

- **Rotate the groups** until all groups have "toured" each chart. When students return to their seats, allow some time for discussion and reactions.

Variations

- **Jigsaw Walking Tour** - If time to tour is limited, form groups made up of the same number of students as there are charts around the room (4 charts means there should be 4 members in a group). Have group members number off and send one representative to each chart. Students form new groups at the charts and react. They then return to their original groups to take turns reporting on the information on each chart and their reactions to it.

- **Gallery Walk** - Pictures or other works of art are displayed around the room and the students move from display to display responding to questions or statements given as guidelines for analyzing the artwork.

adapted from Chuck Shipp, Fairfax High School, Fairfax, VA

Art Treasure Hunt

Find the artwork that... (Write the title of the work, the artist and date.)

repeats a shape	uses contrast to create interest	uses symbols
illustrates a fable or myth	has a rhythm like a song	is all about color
draws your eyes to one spot	makes you feel confused	is evenly balanced
really seems to move	uses line to create texture	captures a moment from history
tells a story	has very strong feelings behind it	seems to go back in space

Debbie Novak, Evanston Township High School, Evanston, IL

Alternatives to...
Whole Class Question-Answer

...for a More Active & Productive Learning Environment

One of the most frequently used teaching strategies is the Whole Class Question-Answer strategy. The steps are as follows:

1. The teacher asks a question.

2. Students who wish to respond raise their hands.

3. The teacher calls on one student.

4. The student attempts to state the correct answer.

Recognize it? It often starts with **"Who can tell me...?"** Since this strategy (also known as a **recitation**) is used so frequently it is important that we ask ourselves just how effective it is. The bad news about this strategy is that the teacher is really the only one in the classroom actively engaged with all the questions and answers; many students may be simply putting in seat time while a few students answer the questions. For those students who are not auditory learners, the recitation may serve as background noise while they visualize who knows what.

Fortunately, there are many **alternatives to Whole Class Question-Answer;** they include the use of **manipulatives and signal cards, plus the active learning strategies described in this chapter, journal entries, interactive notebooks, slates, white boards, and think pads.** If we really want to engage learners, communicate high expectations, and check for understanding, there are literally hundreds of ways to engage all learners in the process.

Hands on Checking for Understanding

Full Steam Ahead!

Signal Cards

Provide students with cards to signal understanding of concepts, or directions, or a sense of "I'm lost!", and you send the message that it is all right not to understand everything the first time around.

You can use as many cards as you want, but a good place to start is with red, green and yellow cards that have universal meanings.

Students can signal:

> "Stop, I'm lost!" or "Slow down, I'm getting confused" or "Full steam ahead!"

> negative, positive, or zero

> complete, run-on, or fragments of sentences

> saturated, semi-saturated, or unsaturated

Whatever meanings you assign the cards, the possibilities are endless!

Gerry Zeltman, teacher of English at Rush-Henrietta High School in Henrietta, New York reports that his senior students are far more willing to admit confusion and ask questions when they have a set of cards with which to signal. Several elementary teachers suggest that library card pockets taped to the student's desk work well for keeping track of the cards. Pam Lecy, of Appleton Area School District in Wisconsin, reports that she uses narrow cards held together in a fan-like fashion with a brad, numbered 1 through 5. Students signal their responses to questions beamed to the entire class in response to stems such as **"If you think it is a mammal, signal 1." "If you think it is a reptile, signal 2." " If you are not sure, signal 3."** Any meaning can be assigned the cards.

Hands on
Checking for
Understanding

Manipulatives

Manipulatives provide **concrete props for abstract concepts** and objects for **kinesthetic learners** to handle. Elementary math teachers are masters at using math manipulatives and the usefulness of such tools is becoming more known across the profession. Using **Index cards, strips of paper, or cut up transparencies** with words, phrases, events, steps in formulas, translations, etc. printed on them offer students the opportunity to demonstrate understanding of sequences and other relationships in a tactile way. Small globes, **miniature models,** straws, and other objects that can be moved and arranged are also useful in helping students process their learning and demonstrate their understanding.

Sort/Category Cards

A pack of index cards can work miracles in helping you and your students know who knows what! Paper cut to 3x5 size can do the trick but these are much more likely to be torn or wrinkled beyond use in a very short time. Possible uses include:

> **vocabulary terms and definition matching**
> **sequencing historical events or scientific processes**
> **categorizing**
> **"I know." "I sort of know," and "I haven't a clue" piles**

In addition to their usefulness as a way to check for understanding, once the cards are made, they can be used in dozens of ways such as for **Inside-Outside Circles** or **I Have the Question, Who Has the Answer,** as entries in class graphic organizers, and for student created games.

Checking for Understanding

with Written Responses:

Slates, White Boards, & Think Pads

Widely used for many years in elementary classrooms, these **individual response formats** are used with increasing frequency in secondary classrooms. Teachers in all disciplines are finding that these tools provide explicit evidence of student understanding during the learning process and promote active participation by all students.

Johnson (1982) requires his high school math students to have their **think pads** and pencils ready for use throughout the entire instructional period. During his math classes, he asks students to "Write the factors of 36" and then circulates around the classroom to see who has written what. It is clear that he finds out much more about who can factor 36 than he would if he stood in the front of the room and asked, "Who can tell me the factors of 36?"

These **think pads** are created by using recycled worksheets cut into quarters and stapled together as small pads of paper. **Slates and white boards** can be ordered from educational supply catalogs. You can also find lightweight laminated cardboard versions in teacher supply stores. **Dry erase markers** must be used on the white boards and a small **square of felt** works well as an eraser.

This kind of checking can be done frequently throughout the explanation of any multi-step process. Asking for student response after almost each teacher statement provides an opportunity to identify where and with whom the learning breaks down.

Checking for understanding in this way, before students do homework or other independent practice, helps ensure that the students are not practicing errors or experiencing frustration during their independent work.

As a **variation,** you can engage students in helping with the checking process by assigning the same problem to all students. As a student finishes, she signals for the teacher to check her work. If it is correct, this student and others who follow can join the teacher in checking the work of others. This shortens the process and gives all students a chance to successfully complete the practice problem before moving on to the next step.

Assignments

Assignments

Skill Building | V | Meaning Making

TOP TEN QUESTIONS
to ask myself as I design lessons

1. What should **students know and be able to do** with what they know as a result of this lesson? How are these objectives related to national, state, and/or district standards or proficiencies?

2. How will **students demonstrate what they know and what they can do** with what they know? What will be the **assessment criteria** and what form will it take?

3. How will **I find out** what **students already know,** and how will I help them access what they know and have experienced both inside and outside the classroom? How will **I help them** not only **build on prior experiences** but **deal with misconceptions** and **reframe their thinking** when appropriate?

4. How will new knowledge, concepts, and skills be introduced? Given the diversity of my students, what are **my best options for sources and presentation modes** of new material?

5. How will I facilitate student processing (meaning making) of new information or processes? What are the key questions, activities, and assignments (in class or homework)?

6. How will **I check for student understanding** during the lesson?

7. What do I need to do to **differentiate instruction** so that the learning experiences are productive for all students?

8. How will I **"Frame the Learning"** so that **students know the objectives**, the **rationale** for the objectives and activities, the directions and procedures, as well as the **assessment criteria** at the beginning of the learning process?

9. How will I build in opportunities for students to make real world connections and to learn and use the varied and complex thinking skills they need to succeed in the classroom and the world beyond?

10. What adjustments need to be made in the **learning environment** so that we can work and learn efficiently during this study?

Awe-Inspiring
Assignments & Assessments

Issues to Consider and Communicate to Students:

A CLEAR STATEMENT OF THE TASK What am I supposed to do?

THE SPECIFIC PURPOSE OF THE TASK Why do I have to do this?

THE RELATION OF THE ASSIGNMENT OR ASSESSMENT TO THE COURSE OBJECTIVES
What does this have to do with what I am supposed to be learning in this class?

THE RELATION OF THE ASSIGNMENT OR ASSESSMENT TO LIFE BEYOND THE CLASSROOM
What does this have to do with anything?

AUDIENCE FOR THE RESPONSE
Who, other than my teacher and I, might be interested in, benefit or learn from the work I do?

KINDS OF THINKING REQUIRED
What kind of thinking will I have to do in order to complete this?

OPTIONS OR CHOICES FOR RESPONSE
What choices do I have? What if...?

WORKING CONDITIONS
- Individual or group work identified. If group work, roles identified as appropriate.
- Materials, equipment, or resources available to students.
- Administrative constraints communicated: time line, order of tasks, how to obtain help and get questions answered.

How and with whom am I supposed to work?

ASSESSMENT STANDARDS AND CRITERIA
How will I know when I am finished and that I have done it right?

- Be sure students have the **prerequisite skills** and **knowledge** to successfully complete the assignment.
- Provide **models** of new behaviors, processes, and products.
- Identify **potential pitfalls** by doing a task analysis or by completing the assignment following the directions exactly as you have written them.

Project Power

Points to Consider

- Identify **standards, curriculum, thinking skills and process objectives** to be incorporated into projects.

- Design and distribute **assessment criteria** to students at the beginning of the process.

- Decide whether to let students design projects based on their **interest** within the parameters established by the standards or to plan them yourself to match the standards.

- Decide whether students will work **alone or in groups** and what **choices** they will have about working conditions.

- Establish clear and reasonable **timelines.**

- Do a **task analysis** to identify potential problem areas and decide what to do to deal with these issues.

- Plan frequency of the **progress reports** based on the age, experience, and skill level of students. Design "benchmarks" where students check in with you or the project leaders. These can include not only what has been accomplished, but past and potential pitfalls, and plans for the next phase of the project.

Potential Final Product Problems

- **Oral Reports:** A series of oral reports can be deadly unless some clear elements of creativity are built into them. Consider having students make videotapes or newscasts that can be shared with others.

- **Copy Work:** Rather than having students "report on" a given topic, have them react to or create something related to the topic. Tasks such as interviews, murals, debates, or presentations to other groups produce more thinking and more enthusiasm for the project.

Helpful Habits

- **Directions:** All multi-step directions are best communicated in writing.

- **Models:** Keep exceptional student projects from year to year to use as models...or videotape presentations to use as models.

- **Audiences:** As often as possible, have the students present or share their projects with audiences beyond the classroom.

See page 129 for the RAFT format that can be used for long term projects and Chapter VII for lists of potential products, perspectives and audiences.

Problems of the 90s Invention Convention
An English & Math Interdisciplinary Project

Purpose

- To integrate English and math skills into a real world project
- To engage learners in using basic skills in a meaningful project based assignment

Process

- Students identify a task that is difficult for them or others to do.
- Students choose a project and solution that is realistic and acceptable for a school project.
- Have students brainstorm problems and possible solutions.
- Students may work with a partner or alone.

The Project

- Create a colorful, neat, schematic, **scaled drawing** of the invention on poster board.
- Create a **scale model** of the invention in a box no larger than that which would be used for Xerox paper.
- Write a **description of the invention** and how it works. Note any **math and/or physics** formulas and their applications.
- Write a **description of the benefits** of the invention. (i.e. cost saving, time saving).
- Design a full color **newspaper/magazine ad** for the invention.
- Create a **one minute television or radio commercial** for the invention.
- Write a **newspaper feature article** about the inventor(s) and invention.
- Prepare a **five minute speech** about the invention following the **"rules for speech making"** taught in class. An **outline for the speech** must be prepared and handed in for assessment.

Linda Karl and Ray Kropp, Polaris High School, District 218, Oaklawn, IL

Investigations into Unusual Units of Measurement

Throughout our short unit on the Customary Unit of Measurement (the measurement system used most often in the United States), we will be focusing on the units typically used every day. However, there are many **UNUSUAL UNITS OF MEASUREMENT** that are used by a variety of people in their jobs and/or hobbies.

Your research should answer the following questions:

1. What is your unit of measure?
2. What does your unit measure (length, area, volume, capacity, weight, frequency, speed, amount, etc.)?
3. What specific item or purpose is it used for?
4. What is its size definition and/or relationship to other units?
5. What profession or person may use your unit of measure?
6. What are other interesting facts or history about your unit of measure?
7. List your resource (where you received your information).

Reporting Your Findings:

You may use any material available in school to report your research. You may use a computer to type your project (as long as you do the computer work). However, your final project should include written answers or diagrams to the questions 1-6 above.

Materials available: chart paper, white/colored plain ditto paper, construction paper, overhead materials... ask me and I'll see what I can do!!!

Oral Report: Be ready to present on _____. Using the written part of your project, prepare a brief report (1-2 minutes) to the class based on your research on your unusual unit of measure.

Chris Regelsberger, West Irondequoit Schools, Rochester, NY

Cord
Hogshead
Peck
Carat
Karat
Watt
Bolt
Barrel
Horsepower
Calorie
Rod
Furlong
Hand
Acre
Board Foot
Ream
Hertz
Gross Tonnage
Mach 1
Light Year
Jigger
Gill
Troy Pound
Knot
Quire
Gross
Bit
Nose
Magnum
Lux
Btu
Ampere
Volt
Dram
Rick
Hectare
Byte
Shot
Pica
RPM
Bushel
Mole
Fortnight
Eon
Fathom
Franc
Era
R Factor
Score
Pennyweight
Scruple
Decibel
Farthing
G Force

Howard Gardner's Multiple Intelligence Theory

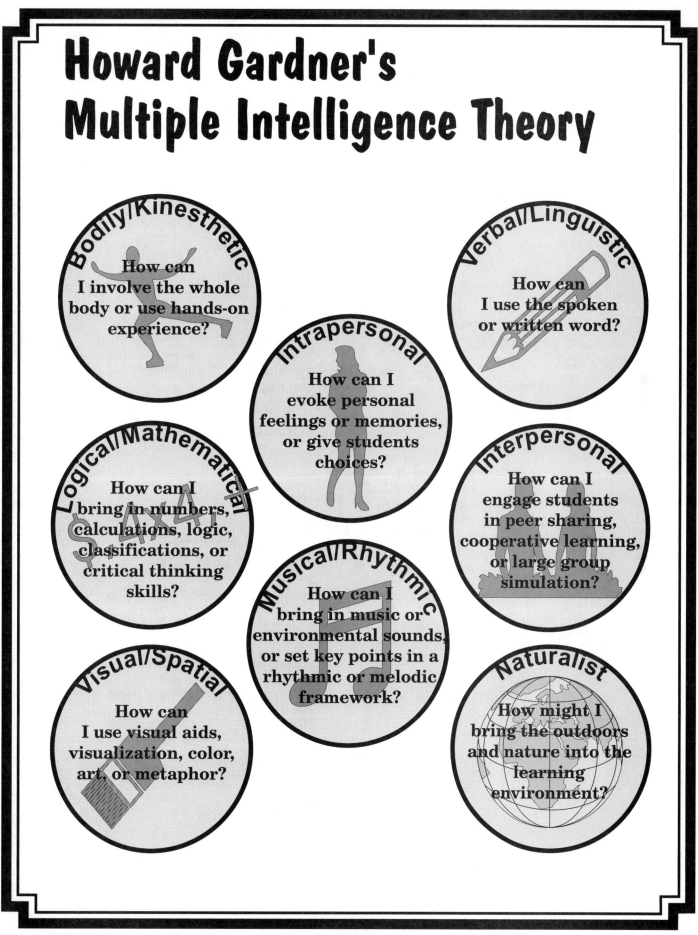

Bodily/Kinesthetic
How can I involve the whole body or use hands-on experience?

Verbal/Linguistic
How can I use the spoken or written word?

Intrapersonal
How can I evoke personal feelings or memories, or give students choices?

Logical/Mathematical
How can I bring in numbers, calculations, logic, classifications, or critical thinking skills?

Interpersonal
How can I engage students in peer sharing, cooperative learning, or large group simulation?

Musical/Rhythmic
How can I bring in music or environmental sounds, or set key points in a rhythmic or melodic framework?

Visual/Spatial
How can I use visual aids, visualization, color, art, or metaphor?

Naturalist
How might I bring the outdoors and nature into the learning environment?

Strategies for the Multiple Intelligences

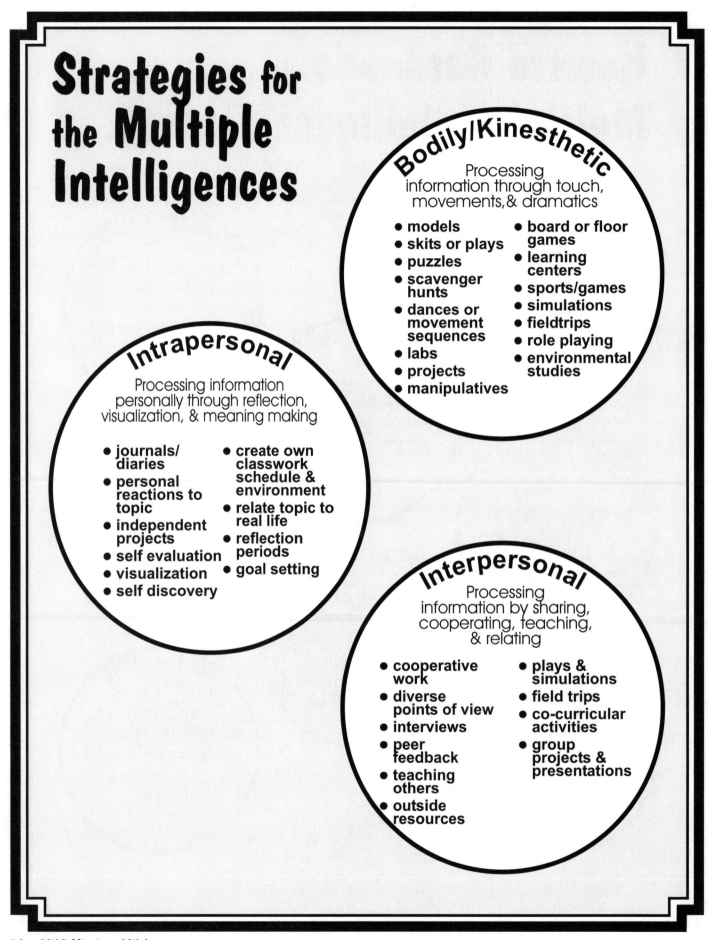

Bodily/Kinesthetic
Processing information through touch, movements, & dramatics

- models
- skits or plays
- puzzles
- scavenger hunts
- dances or movement sequences
- labs
- projects
- manipulatives
- board or floor games
- learning centers
- sports/games
- simulations
- fieldtrips
- role playing
- environmental studies

Intrapersonal
Processing information personally through reflection, visualization, & meaning making

- journals/diaries
- personal reactions to topic
- independent projects
- self evaluation
- visualization
- self discovery
- create own classwork schedule & environment
- relate topic to real life
- reflection periods
- goal setting

Interpersonal
Processing information by sharing, cooperating, teaching, & relating

- cooperative work
- diverse points of view
- interviews
- peer feedback
- teaching others
- outside resources
- plays & simulations
- field trips
- co-curricular activities
- group projects & presentations

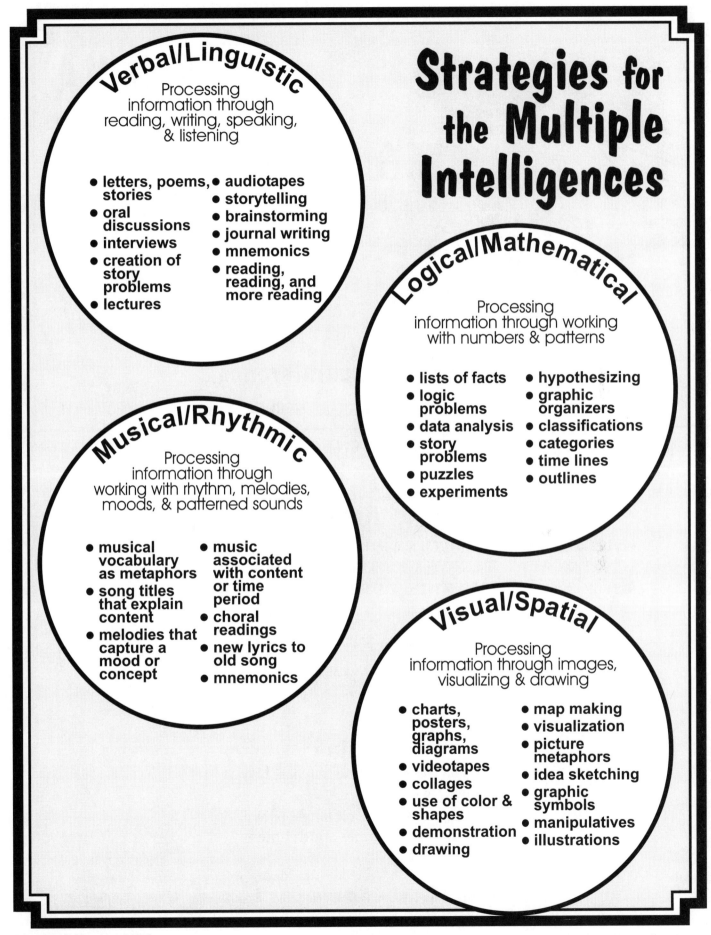

Strategies for the Multiple Intelligences

Verbal/Linguistic

Processing information through reading, writing, speaking, & listening

- letters, poems, stories
- oral discussions
- interviews
- creation of story problems
- lectures
- audiotapes
- storytelling
- brainstorming
- journal writing
- mnemonics
- reading, reading, and more reading

Logical/Mathematical

Processing information through working with numbers & patterns

- lists of facts
- logic problems
- data analysis
- story problems
- puzzles
- experiments
- hypothesizing
- graphic organizers
- classifications
- categories
- time lines
- outlines

Musical/Rhythmic

Processing information through working with rhythm, melodies, moods, & patterned sounds

- musical vocabulary as metaphors
- song titles that explain content
- melodies that capture a mood or concept
- music associated with content or time period
- choral readings
- new lyrics to old song
- mnemonics

Visual/Spatial

Processing information through images, visualizing & drawing

- charts, posters, graphs, diagrams
- videotapes
- collages
- use of color & shapes
- demonstration
- drawing
- map making
- visualization
- picture metaphors
- idea sketching
- graphic symbols
- manipulatives
- illustrations

SCHOOL BUS

FORMULA FOLLIES

Multiple Intelligences Example

Sing to the tune of "Wheels on the Bus"

Perimeter/Circumference

For **perimeter** of a figure you ADD THE SIDES,
ADD THE SIDES, ADD THE SIDES
For **perimeter** of a figure you ADD THE SIDES,
All the way around!

Circumference of a circle is π x d,
π x d, π x d,
Circumference of a circle is π x d,
π is 3.14!

Area

Area of a rectangle is LENGTH x WIDTH,
LENGTH x WIDTH, LENGTH x WIDTH,
Area of a rectangle is LENGTH x WIDTH,
only for this shape!

Area of a triangle is 1/2 bh,
1/2 bh, 1/2 bh,
Area of a triangle is 1/2 bh,
that's 1/2 times base times height!

Area of a circle is πr2, πr2, πr2,
Area of a circle is πr2, that's π x r x r!

Volume

The **volume** of a rectangle is lwh,
lwh, lwh,
The **volume** of a rectangle is lwh,
that's length times width times height!

Sue Quinn & Joanne Fusare-White, Roth Middle School, Rush-Henrietta Schools, Henrietta, NY

Reading Project Choices

After you have read your novel, review this list of projects and select one. Fill out and return the attached contract to me no later than February 22. If none of the projects suit you, feel free to design one of your own. Don't forget to choose a project that showcases your strengths. Projects may be passed in from March 8 through March 15.

Kinesthetic:

1. Make a life-sized paper-stuffed person found in your novel.
2. Draw a scale model of something from the novel you read.
3. Build a relief map of the setting of the story.
4. Construct a building from your novel.
5. Act out a scene from the novel you read.
6. Choreograph a dance that shows the theme, the development of a character, or a scene from the book you read.
7. Design and make a quilt/wall hanging that depicts your novel in some way.

Verbal/Linguistic:

1. Choose a major character from the book. Focus in on a crucial time in the book and create a diary that the character would have written.
2. Put together a cast for the film version of the book. Imagine the director-producer wants a casting director to make recommendations. Decide who would be the actors and actresses. Include photos and descriptions of the "stars" and tell why each is perfect for the part.
3. Write a collection of poems that show different aspects of the novel: the characters, the setting, the plot, the climax, the theme...
4. Write a newspaper article about an important event from the book you read.
5. Write the next chapter in the novel.

Intrapersonal:

1. Relate a character's development to your own life history. This can be done through writing, drawing or other means.
2. Relate a hobby or interest that you might have to the novel you read.
3. Create an individual project that "shows" your feelings about the book.

Logical/Sequential:

1. Choose an automobile from the story you read. Find out as much as you can about the car, especially how the engine works.
2. Create a code that the characters in the story could use to communicate.
3. Develop a logic puzzle or brain teaser based on something that happened in the book.
4. Set up a "what if" experiment to see what would happen if "this" didn't happen.
5. Make up a strategy game based on the book you read.
6. Create a flowchart/concept map that shows the major players in the book you read.
7. Write equations that describe the characters in the story.

Rhythmic:

1. Write a rap or a song about your book.
2. Create a discography that represents the book: the setting, the characters, the conflict, the plot, the climax, the theme.
3. What musical instruments would the characters play? What type of music would they listen to?
4. *The Outsiders*: watch the movie. If it were your job to change it to a musical, where in the story would singing be appropriate? Who would sing and what would the song be about? (*West Side Story*)

Visual:

1. Think about the book you read. Find a comfortable place and doodle. Reflect on your doodles and see what story they tell about the novel you read. Report on your findings with a mini-exhibition.
2. Use a camera or camcorder to create a collage of the book.
3. Which geometric figures describe the characters in the book? Create something visual to represent these ideas.
4. What colors do the characters represent? Create an exhibition which shows the colors of the characters.

Interpersonal:

1. Find a guest speaker to talk to the class about a topic addressed in the book you read.
2. Plan a party for a character in the novel. You need invitations, decorations, food, music, etc.
3. Mediate a problem between two characters in the book. What would your advice be?
4. Introduce one of your friends to one of the characters in the book. With which characters would your friends be comfortable? Why?

Wendy Govoni, Holderness Central School, Holderness, NH

Everything's Up to Date in Kansas City...Or is it?

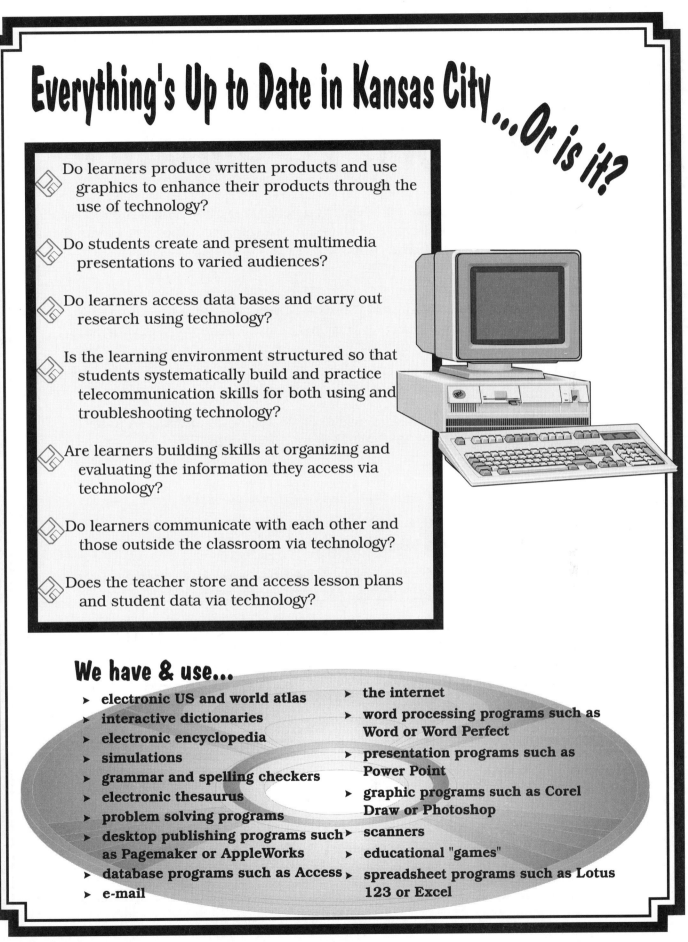

◇ Do learners produce written products and use graphics to enhance their products through the use of technology?

◇ Do students create and present multimedia presentations to varied audiences?

◇ Do learners access data bases and carry out research using technology?

◇ Is the learning environment structured so that students systematically build and practice telecommunication skills for both using and troubleshooting technology?

◇ Are learners building skills at organizing and evaluating the information they access via technology?

◇ Do learners communicate with each other and those outside the classroom via technology?

◇ Does the teacher store and access lesson plans and student data via technology?

We have & use...

- ➤ **electronic US and world atlas**
- ➤ **interactive dictionaries**
- ➤ **electronic encyclopedia**
- ➤ **simulations**
- ➤ **grammar and spelling checkers**
- ➤ **electronic thesaurus**
- ➤ **problem solving programs**
- ➤ **desktop publishing programs such as Pagemaker or AppleWorks**
- ➤ **database programs such as Access**
- ➤ **e-mail**

- ➤ **the internet**
- ➤ **word processing programs such as Word or Word Perfect**
- ➤ **presentation programs such as Power Point**
- ➤ **graphic programs such as Corel Draw or Photoshop**
- ➤ **scanners**
- ➤ **educational "games"**
- ➤ **spreadsheet programs such as Lotus 123 or Excel**

Biography
PowerPoint Presentation

You are to prepare a 3-5 minute oral report on your biography. The outline of your PowerPoint presentation will help you select and present the important events from your book. You may use additional props if you wish to do so.

Requirements:

Title Slide: Include the title and author of the book you read (and the name of the subject of the biography if that isn't clear from the title). Also include your name.

5 Content Slides: Think of the content slides as an outline of your subject. The title should be a broader-based topic, while the bulleted points will be sub-points. These should all relate to each other.

Visual Appeal of Screen: Plan for effective use of color, text font, and size. You are encouraged to include graphics to enhance your presentation.

  Color: Choose background colors that contrast highly with the text.

  Text Font and Size: Choose a text font at least 36 points or larger.

  Graphics: Choose clip art graphics that are appropriate to your text.
  Remember: Graphics should enhance, not distract!

Suzanne Kisielica, Special Education Department, New Trier High School, Winnetka, IL

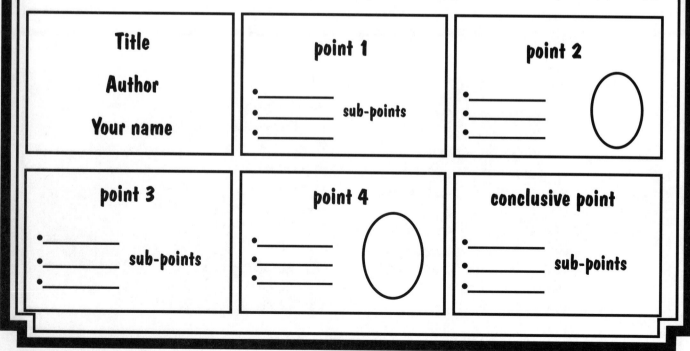

TV Time

Your Assignment

You and your partner will take a survey to determine how much TV your classmates and other teenage friends watch on a daily basis. You will have to determine ways to collect the data. Here are some questions for you to consider before you begin:

◇ How can you be sure your information is accurate?

◇ Do you expect the results will be the same from one week to the next, or will there be some variation? Why?

◇ Will the results depend on the month? Why?

◇ Is it necessary to keep track of all 7 days, or will the results be the same from one day to the next?

The "Deliverables"

To receive credit for this assignment, you must submit the following:

• A copy of a survey given to at least 10 people (outside of this class). The only restriction is that the students must be between the ages of 13 and 18.

• A set of 1-4 bar graphs or other charts summarizing the results of the data. The graphs and charts can be hand-drawn or computer-generated. I can show you how to generate graphs on the computer. The only restriction is that the graphs and charts be neat, accurate, and legible.

• A brief written analysis of survey data, not to exceed one page (8 1/2 x 11). This submission must be typed.

TV Time continued...

Today you have two options on how to spend your 40 minutes:

* Type up your survey of TV viewing habits.
* Complete an exercise to show you how to create charts and graphs on the computer.
    1. If you want to type your survey, you will use Microsoft Word. It is located in the Microsoft Office directory.
    2. If you want to create charts and graphs, you will use Microsoft powerpoint. This package is also located in the Microsoft Office directory. I have given you some sample data, as well as two examples of the charts that you may want to create during class. I will give you some instructions to get started on the bar chart. You will create the pie chart on your own.

To create the bar chart:

1. Determine how I calculated the average hours/day of viewing for cable subscribers vs. non-cable subscribers.
2. Click on the PowerPoint icon to use the software.
3. Create a new slide.
4. Select an Auto Layout option. You will select the bar chart with a title.
5. Enter the title.
6. Double-click on the graph to create it. A data sheet wall paper will appear, containing some sample data. You will need to replace the sample data with your data.
7. Once you enter the data, close the data sheet. A first draft of your graph will appear. If it does not look perfect yet, do not worry! It is normal procedure to have to edit the chart.
8. In order to edit your graph/chart, double-click on the graph itself. A new set of buttons appears on the top of the screen. These will help you to complete the editing.

I WILL BE AROUND TO GIVE YOU HELP!

Once you complete the first graph, you may do one of the following:

* Create the second slide from the packet.
* Use data from your surveys to create one of the assigned graphs, due next week.

You can drop into the math lab between now and next Friday during any period except 6th.

Good Luck!

Terry Phillips, New Trier High School, Winnetka, IL

Role
Audience
Form
Time

The **RAFT** technique, which is explained in many journals and attributed to various sources, requires students to create scenarios about the content being studied. **RAFT** allows students to consider the information from a variety of perspectives and to use a wide range of formats to present information to limitless audiences. This brain compatible approach causes students to rethink, rewrite, and discuss an event or concept in another place or time or through the eyes or voice of the famous or familiar. The lists of potential products and perspectives listed on pages 175 through 186 provide a multitude of possibilities.

You, as a fourth grade teacher, are to write test questions on the _____. Write one question for each paragraph, using either true-false, multiple-choice, fill-in-the-blank, or matching format. Provide the answers and sign your name. You will exchange questions with Mr. Oliver's class tomorrow.

You are a political cartoonist for the *Washington Post* newspaper. Design two cartoons that illustrate a "hot" issue related to our unit on Immigration. Prepare one to represent the issue in the early 1900s and one from a current perspective. Include captions and your signature as the artist.

Pretend you are a visitor from Ukraine. Write a three to five paragraph letter to your family back home describing how Chicago is like Kiev.

Assume that one of your classmates has been absent for all of our study of the circulatory system. Use the list of potential products to design a specific product that will describe in detail how the system works. Remember this student missed the entire unit! Spend some time thinking about what are the most important things to include.

Role
Audience
Form
Time

R - You are a volunteer for the Bull Moose (Progressive) Party

A - You are trying to attract Republicans to join the party

F - Produce a campaign poster

T - 1912 - Election Year

Bull Moose	President	Democratic
Teddy Roosevelt	William H. Taft	Woodrow Wilson

Joyce Nagle, Irondequoit High School, West Irondeqoit Central School District, Rochester, NY

"TEEN HEALTH HABITS"

Directions: Imagine that you are a newspaper journalist for the **Rochester Democrat & Chronicle** and you have an assignment to do an article about teen health habits for the **"flipside"** column that appears in every Monday's paper. In order to do this, you need some research so...

Conduct a survey in which you will:

a.   **Interview** 6 students not in this class.

b.   Choose the students from **two different age groups:**

       10-12, 13-15, 16-18.

c.   **Ask** the students privately, at a time when they can think.

d.   You can ask the students and fill in their answers or you can have them **fill in the answers** for themselves.

e.   After completing your survey, **show the main similarities and differences** by filling in the graphic organizer (Venn diagram) or making a spreadsheet on the computer.

f.   Using the answers from your survey, **write an article** for "flipside" about teen health habits and what influences the health of teens in the '90s.

Judy White, Roth Middle School, Rush-Henrietta Schools, Henrietta, NY

Ready! Set!! RAFTs Away!!!

Directions: Choose your **RAFT** and head out on an exciting adventure! You are invited to become a character from *The Hundred Dresses.*

RAFT 1:

You are **Wanda Petronski**. Write a **persuasive letter** to **Maddie** to convince her that she made the right decision when she vowed never again to stand by and say nothing when someone was being made fun of. You must convince her with three strong points.

RAFT 2:

You are **Wanda Petronski**. Write a **persuasive letter** to **Maddie and/or Peggy** to convince them that it is important to treat others with kindness and respect. You must convince them, with three strong points, to live by "The Golden Rule" and treat others the way you want to be treated.

RAFT 3:

You are **Maddie or Peggy.** Write a **letter to Wanda** asking for her forgiveness and ask her to come back to school. You must convince her that things will be different if she returns. You must **persuade** her to return using at least three good reasons.

RAFT 4:

You are **Maddie.** You have finally gathered the courage to write a **persuasive letter to Peggy** with the hope of convincing her to treat others with respect and kindness. You hope to show her that she will be a better person if she changes her ways. Persuade her to change her ways!

RAFT 5:

Create your own scenario. Take on **any role** you choose and identify your **audience**. The form must be a persuasive letter. You can base the situation on a classroom from today or fifty years ago like Room 13.

Michelle Flood, West Irondequoit Central School District, Rochester, NY

You are the proud owner of a sporting goods company that specializes in the manufacturing of **tennis rackets, basketballs, bicycles and baseballs.** Your business is so successful that you also export goods to **France, Great Britain, Japan and Russia.** Next month you are offering a special promotion of your goods. You want to make sure your prices are consistent in each of the countries where you do business. Use the **February 1996 Foreign Exchange Rates** to determine the prices for your goods.

Foreign Exchange Rates

(Value of 1 U.S. dollar in February, 1996)

Country	Value
France	5.55 francs
Great Britain	.62 pounds
Russia	5626 rubles
Japan	120.95 yen

	A	B	C	D	E	F
1		U.S. Dollars	Francs	Pounds	Rubles	Yen
2	Tennis racket	85				
3	Basketball	29				
4	Bicycle	335				
5	Baseball	5				

Christine Regelsberger, West Irondequoit Central School District, Rochester, NY

Building Your Own RAFT

Role _____

Audience _____

Form (product) _____

Time _____

Role _____

Audience _____

Form (product) _____

Time _____

Role _____

Audience _____

Form (product) _____

Time _____

Homework

homework (noun):   **1.** carefully planned and meaningful work completed by students outside of the class period where it is assigned.   **2.** outside of class work for which students have prerequisite skills and are able to complete independently.

Categories of Homework Assignments

Practice Homework...

helps students master skills and reinforce in-class learning; can be boring and repetitive.   Unless we differentiate homework assignments, it is guaranteed that some students are wasting time practicing something they have already mastered and that some are trying to practice something they have not yet learned.   Practice homework should be given only when it is clear that the learner can work with the skill independently.   Avoid repetitiveness of practice homework by giving students the five most difficult problems to do. If they can successfully complete those, they do not need to do the easier problems. Better yet, let students identify the practice exercises they need to do; both teacher and student track the effectiveness of that practice and adjust as necessary.

Extension Homework...

helps students take what they learn and connect it with real life.   This type of homework often gives students the option to choose their method of gathering data, processing learning and demonstrating learning.

Preparation Homework...

prepares students for upcoming lesson or unit.   Reading a chapter on material to be covered in class is not good preparation homework.   Reading research clearly indicates that comprehension is low if the students have no prior experiences with and/or discussions about the topic.   Reading chapters is best assigned following classwork.

Creative Homework...

helps students integrate multiple concepts (possibly from more than one curricular area); often presented in the form of long term projects.   Students should be asked to react to rather than report on what they are learning. This promotes development of critical thinking and problem solving skills.

This classification system (Lee & Pruitt, 1979) makes it clear that most of the homework we assign falls in the practice and preparation categories.   Common sense and our own experiences as learners tell us that extension and creative homework assignments are much more likely to engage students in the learning and minimize the ever present problems of incomplete or copied homework.

Homework continued...
Examples of Each Category of Homework

Practice
- most questions at the end of the chapter
- vocabulary drill
- memorization of (hopefully important) facts
- calculations

Extension
- RAFT assignments (p. 129)
- higher levels of Bloom's Taxonomy (p. 231)
- Williams' Taxonomy assignments (p. 235)
- daily journal writing from thought provoking stems
- interactive notebooks (p. 227)
- locate real world situations where the knowledge and skills students are learning are used.

Preparation
- review of past related topics
- pre-tests
- surveys
- read the chapter prior to any discussion

Creative
- projects...especially involving student choice and interdisciplinary links
- performance assessment tasks

Practice/Creative Mix
- Have students complete a limited number of questions/ problems. Then have them create several problems or questions using the same content or skills.

IN CASE OF STUDENT/TEACHER AGGRAVATION, CHECK FOR:

- Unplanned or irrelevant homework. Perhaps there is a homework policy and you feel compelled to assign something even when it isn't appropriate.
- Assignments given at the very end of class with no time for clarifying purposes or explanations of confusing directions.
- Assignments that seem like busy work and aren't moving students closer to competency with the standard on which they are working. They may already know how to do what they are being asked to do or this type of activity hasn't been productive in the past.
- Assignments which call for knowledge and skills not currently in the students' repertoire and there is little chance for success.

Homework continued...
Assigning Meaningful & Productive Homework

- Include **choice** and **variety** in homework assignments

- Review the assignment before giving it to students. Identify major concepts and important vocabulary. **Anticipate difficulties** and **prepare students** to deal with them.

- Design assignments that should yield a **success rate** of at least **80-90%**. If students have not mastered the basic concepts, do not give them an assignment that will send them home to work incorrectly.

- When students have difficulty with an assignment, **teaching has to take place** before they are asked to do more of the same work.

- Present assignment in such a way that there is time to **clarify instructions**.

- Give the assignment **orally** and in **writing**. Use a **consistent**, easily seen **location** to **post** assignments.

- Have students keep a **homework log** containing each assignment's directions, connection to the learning objective, and completion time, or the reason why it wasn't completed.

- Have students keep a **learning log** containing a list of assignments, reflections on the learning process, and content. If the assignment is incomplete, have them enter what they tried and where the process broke down. Log entries may be accepted as an alternative to the regular assignment as a good faith effort to learn through trial & error.

- **Avoid assignments such as**:

  "*Read Chapter 3*" (students may read the chapter without purpose or comprehension) and "*Read Chapter 3 and answer the questions at the end of the chapter*" (students may complete the assignment without comprehending a word).

  Instead use "Read Chapter 3 and identify the three most significant factors related to ___. Be prepared to discuss these factors and your rationale for selecting them as the most significant with your discussion groups at the beginning of class tomorrow." This communicates what success looks like and gives a purpose to the work outside of class.

- Give assignments for explicit instructional purposes, **not for punishment**. Do not excuse students from homework for good behavior.

- Plan homework assignments at least a week in advance and **give students a schedule for the week** so they can **allocate** their available **work time**.

Homework continued...

Minimize the Grading of Homework!

At the beginning of the instructional period, have the students work in pairs or groups to **reach consensus on practice homework**. When students cannot agree, they should circle any points of confusion or disagreement. You circulate and intervene with the small groups as necessary. Only mass confusion is dealt with in large group. When papers are collected, they are all correct. The students have done the work and you have no papers to correct!

There is no need to "test" students on facts they have to memorize. Instead have the students **draw the objects or some graphic representation of the facts** to be memorized as a homework assignment. Have the students exchange drawings and label those of a classmate. Students check each other's work. This practice can continue until the tidbits are memorized and can be used later for cumulative review. If drawing won't work, just have the students **create mini-tests or flash cards** to teach and test each other. There are no papers to grade!

When students **write a summary statement** of their thinking or of their readings as a homework assignment, have two students meet to **share their summaries** and to combine their thinking into one paper. **The consensus paper is collected.** The number of papers to be collected is cut in half!

When teaching a new operation in math, a new sentence structure, a new science concept, have students **make up one to five problems that illustrate the new information as homework.** When they arrive in class, have them exchange problems or you can collect them at the door and redistribute them randomly. They work the problems they have received and the problems are returned to the creators for checking and correction. Once again, no papers for you to grade!

2nd Grade Homework

The purpose of homework is to develop responsibility and to enhance learning through daily practice at home. Please encourage your child to develop good study habits by providing a quiet place to work and always taking time to do his/her best. Please check your child's work over and sign your acceptance.

Monday

1. Language Arts: Practice alphabetical order by putting this week's spelling words in your book in alphabetical order.

2. Math: Do practice paper. Next, on the back of the worksheet, write a problem about the score of a game between two teams.

3. Reading: Continue to read your mystery. When you finish one book, begin a new mystery. List the main characters and the main problem in your book.

Tuesday

1. Language Arts: Practice your spelling words by practicing writing good cursive with any ten words from the list.

2. Math: Do practice paper, then write a problem on the back about the score between two soccer teams who scored a combined total of 7 goals.

3. Reading: Before you continue your mystery, write a paragraph about what you think will happen next. Use examples from the book to tell why you predict what you do.

Wednesday

1. Language Arts: Choose 5 spelling words to which you could add suffixes. Add a suffix to each word.

2. Math: Do practice paper and then write a problem on the back involving the use of money.

3. Reading: Continue to read your mystery. Then choose 4 new words you have learned in this book and use each in a sentence.

Thursday

1. Language Arts: Practice your spelling words by writing any 10 of them in cursive 2 times.

2. Math: Do practice paper. Solve this problem on the back of your worksheet. First, you have to make up the data for the problem. Pete went to the store with $8.00. He bought two new books for school. How much money did he spend? Solve.

3. Reading: Read your new chapter book for 20 minutes. Write a paragraph to tell how they are trying to solve the mystery.

Friday   Enjoy your weekend!

Pat Donegan, West Irondequoit Central School District, Rochester, NY

HOMEWORK: 4th Grade Reading

Your monthly reading homework includes reading **two books and completing a project on each.**

First, **read a book of your choice for at least 30 minutes each day**, as time permits with other family activities. You may read more one day and less another. Choose books from a variety of different genres. Keep a record of your reading in your homework journal and hand it in each week on your assigned day.

Second, **you are responsible for completing two of the projects from the list of choices in your homework journal by the end of each month**. New choices will be added each month. You may only use a choice once. This means that when you complete a book, you will choose one of the activities from the list, do the project, and hand it in. You will need to plan your time throughout the month so that you will be sure to complete the two required books and projects. One plan would be to do your reading during the week, and work on your projects on those cold, gray winter days on the weekend. You will need to work out the plan that is best for you. (See next page for list of choices.)

If you have an idea for a project that is not on the list, let me know and we will discuss it.

If you would rather write responses to your reading in your journal as you have in the past, rather than do the projects, you may continue to do so.

Please cut off, sign, and return.

- -

I have read the homework assignment and discussed a plan for successful completion of the homework with my child.

Parent signature _____

Student signature _____

Jean Blakley and Karen Kessler, Honeoye Falls-Lima School District, NY

4th Grade Reading Homework Project Choices

- Imagine that you had an opportunity to **interview the author** of your book shortly after it was published. What questions would you ask? (Keep in mind that good interview questions encourage the person to "open up" and talk. Try not to ask questions that would only get one-word answers.) Write at least five good questions. After you have written the questions, write what you think the author might answer.

- **Choose the music** for an existing song or **write a song** using words that show the traits of one of the characters in your book. Record your song on a tape and include a song sheet with the words to the song. You can use a tape and tape recorder from school if you need it.

- A television spin-off is a new television show based on another show. One of the lesser characters from the original show stars in the new show. Pretend that your book is the original show and you have been asked to **write a spin-off series**. Think about the following when you write your ideas:
    - What is the name of the new show?
    - Which character will star in the show?
    - What new characters will be introduced?
    - What will the story of the first show in the series be about?

- **Make a poster** about the main character in your book. Put yourself in the character's place and decide what characteristics, likes and dislikes are important to show on the poster. You may choose to show these things in any creative way you choose. Be sure that when you are finished, someone who has never read the book will have an understanding of your character by looking at the poster.

- **Write a new ending** for the book you have read. In three different paragraphs, include these three things:
    - A brief description of what the book is about
    - Why you would like the ending to be different
    - How you would have written the ending

Jean Blakley and Karen Kessler, Honeoye Falls-Lima School District, NY

Iroquois Indians: Homework Assignments

Demonstrate your understanding of the Iroquois Indians by choosing one activity for each day.

Day 1	Day 2	Day 3
Daily Life		
On a story wheel, illustrate 3 responsibilities of an Iroquois man and 3 responsibilities of an Iroquois woman.	Create a Venn diagram to compare the home of an Iroquois and your family home. Iroquois My Family	Categorize the Iroquois foods into the following food groups: DAIRY, FRUIT, VEGETABLE, MEAT, and SWEETS. Then, in another color, add what you eat in a typical day.
The Home		
Compose a song, create a poem, or sketch a picture showing what you think was the best and worst part in an Iroquois man or woman's day.	Consider the good and bad points of living in an Iroquois home. List them on a T chart. Good | Bad	You are an Iroquois mother. Plan a menu for a typical meal. Illustrate the meal and the household items you might use.
Food		
Create and then role play a scene in which an Iroquois family spends an evening together.	Describe an Iroquois home in pictures or words.	You are opening an Iroquois restaurant. Create a menu for your patrons. You can only serve Iroquois food.

Ann Esch, Rogers School, West Irondequoit Schools, Rochester, NY

Yup, It's Chemistry!

Organize these substances,
Create a data table,
Make a system,
Identify these unknowns,
Categorize these elements,
Classify this matter.

1. Be creative and find any **grouping of items** in your surroundings. That's right, look at your house, in your drawer, wallet, purse, or backpack. Ex.: shoes, desk drawer stuff.

2. **Lay the objects** out in front of you or draw pictures or take photographs to represent the various objects. You want to have the objects represented visually so that you can move them around and arrange and rearrange them.

3. **Arrange these objects both horizontally and vertically** (both across and up and down). This is similar to "the guys" you arranged in class, and remember how you drew in the secret agent.

4. There should be **at least two trends** or other criteria happening horizontally.
   Ex.: the "guys" bodies got thicker as you went across
   the "guys" had more hair as you went across
   the "guys" mouths went from a frown to a smile as you went across

5. There should be **at least two trends** or other criteria happening vertically.
   Ex.: the "guys" had the same body design in their column
   the "guys" arms increased by one arm as you went down the column

6. When you are done arranging the objects, get poster board and glue and put either the objects or pictures of the **objects on the poster board in the order you decide**.

7. On the **back of the poster board, write a description of the order you chose** and share the reasoning behind your organization. Shhh...don't tell anyone the system you chose. See if they can determine the order on their own.

8. This project is worth **250 points** and **you have COMPLETE CONTROL!**

Laura Zboril & Lynn Hiller, New Trier High School, Winnetka, IL

Homework Planning Sheet

Think of a unit you are teaching now or will be teaching in the near future. Focus on the homework assignments you usually give. List them below:

How might you change those assignments to include all four categories of homework assignments?

📖 Practice

💻 Preparation

☎ Extension

✉ Creative

What language could you use to communicate the homework assignments in a way that students know what to do, know why they are doing it, and know when they are successful?

Assessing
with
Balance

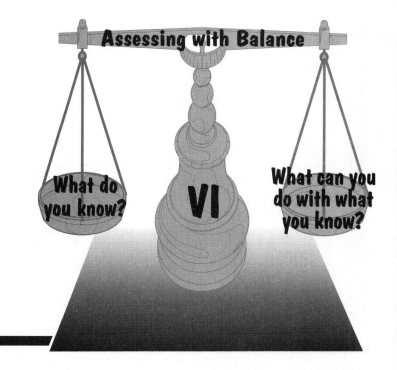

TOP TEN QUESTIONS
to ask myself as I design lessons

1. What should **students know and be able to do** with what they know as a result of this lesson? How are these objectives related to national, state, and/or district standards or proficiencies?

2. How will students demonstrate what they know and what they can do with what they know? What will be the assessment criteria and what form will it take?

3. How will **I find out** what **students already know,** and how will I help them access what they know and have experienced both inside and outside the classroom? How will **I help them** not only **build on prior experiences,** but **deal with misconceptions and reframe their thinking when appropriate?**

4. How will new knowledge, concepts, and skills be introduced? Given the diversity of my students, what are **my best options for sources and presentation modes** of new material?

5. How will I facilitate student processing (meaning making) of new information or processes? What are the key questions, activities, and assignments (in class or homework)?

6. How will **I check for student understanding** during the lesson?

7. What do I need to do to **differentiate instruction** so that the learning experiences are productive for all students?

8. How will I **"Frame the Learning"** so that **students know the objectives,** the **rationale** for the objectives and activities, the directions and procedures, as well as the **assessment criteria** at the beginning of the learning process?

9. How will I build in opportunities for students to make real world connections and to learn and use the varied and complex thinking skills they need to succeed in the classroom and the world beyond?

10. What adjustments need to be made in the **learning environment** so that we can work and learn efficiently during this study?

Best Practice in
Classroom Assessment

Consider whether or not these statements represent your own professional practice. While the term assessment is now used much more than in the past, standard college texts on evaluation of student learning have recommended the following as best practice for decades.

_____ Assessments are used as teaching and learning tools for teacher and students.

Error analysis, that is determining how many students missed which item, has been taught in evaluation and measurement courses for years, yet few of us have become proficient with or committed to such practice. Now the bar is being raised and we are being asked to examine student work collaboratively and to use the data we obtain from student assessment to inform our future teaching practices.

_____ Assessment is an ongoing process that provides formative and summative feedback to students.

Despite our current practice of including homework and class assignments as part of the data we include in determining grades, research clearly states that formative work should not be averaged into a final evaluation of student learning.

_____ Assessments are clearly matched to standards. Both instructional strategies and learning tasks match the standards and the assessment.

Madeline Hunter long advocated for congruency among objectives, lessons and assessment; yet we often, in our harried professional lives, use a publisher's assessments without careful editing. In many instances, students' poor performance on our assessments could be caused by poor assessment design.

_____ Assessment tools are equitable and fair.

Assessments should fairly represent the time spent, the emphasis placed on, and the level of thinking required during the learning process. We need to do a task analysis of test items to identify assumed skills and knowledge. When we identify problem areas, we need to either change the assessment item or provide the needed information or instruction.

Best Practice in
Classroom Assessment continued...

_____ Assessment tools are selected from a wide range of options including, but certainly not limited to, paper and pencil assessments.
Since life is not a "closed book test" our students need multiple opportunities to demonstrate learning in realistic applications. Competency with performance task lists and rubrics allows us to use assessment tools other than paper and pencil assessments with precision because they make the scoring of performance assessment tasks as objective as our scoring of traditional tests.

_____ Assessment criteria clearly communicates how competency or proficiency is to be demonstrated.
While the current emphasis is on using rubrics and performance task lists for performance assessment tasks, the same standard applies to paper and pencil assessments.

_____ Assessment criteria is communicated precisely and publicly prior to students beginning the task.
A review of the literature shows that best practice has always included informing learners of the assessment design and the areas of emphasis in the assessment.

An Assessment Continuum
from Formative to Summative

Preassessments

Checks for Understanding

Observations/Anecdotal Records

Student Questions/Comments (In-class and in Journals)

Teacher Questions & Prompts (In-class)

Assignments (including Homework)

Peer Assessment

Self Assessment

Quizzes

Tests

Performance Tasks (Short and Long Term)

Variations on a theme...
Paper & Pencil Assessment

Designer Assessment
Create a bank of assessment questions or items. This assessment, which includes items totaling two to four hundred points, can be organized around levels of thinking or subsets of the topic being studied. Students choose questions to equal 100 points. Students could have complete free choice as to what to answer or you could designate a certain number of points from each section. Provide space in the margin so that students can keep track of the total points they have attempted to earn. This sort of assessment encourages students to build test taking skills, such as reading through the entire assessment before beginning, deciding what they know, and don't know, and planning use of time.

Front Page News
Put questions that are to be answered by all students on the first page. These questions would represent the most important information that all students need to know at the end of the unit of study. Put the next levels of questions on the following pages and then you and/or students decide which are to be answered. You may stipulate that in order to demonstrate competency students have to correctly answer all the questions on the first page, and failure to do so will result in reteaching, restudy, and retesting on those particular points. Some information is, after all, more important than the rest.

Differentiating the Big One
Design a comprehensive paper and pencil assessment and then circle or otherwise indicate which questions that students are to answer. For example, designate a certain copy of the test for Susan, then circle question numbers to indicate which questions Susan is to answer. You may want to offer Susan the option of trying other questions after she has attempted the teacher selected questions. Grading is done in terms of how Susan did with the questions she was supposed to complete rather than with the entire assessment. This method allows appropriate assessment of students working at different achievement levels without adding a huge amount of preparation time for the teacher.

What I Studied and You Didn't Ask
Include an assessment item that asks students to indicate what information they thought was important or especially interesting that you did not include in the assessment; the item is worth x points toward the total score. This builds in a relief valve for students, gives them a sense of efficacy and gives the teacher important information about what students considered important or interesting.

Consensus Testing
Students work through problems individually and record personal answers. They then work in groups of two or three to compare answers and reach consensus about best answer or most important points to include. If you value assessment as a real learning opportunity for students, this method promotes that continued learning, and it simulates real world situations in which students will have to listen to the ideas of others in "stressful" situations.

Best Test
Students create a test, complete with answers, for the unit of study. You and/or a committee of students review the tests and decide which one best assesses important ideas and is best constructed. The class takes the test and the test designers earn their grade for designing the test. For this method to be as productive as possible, some teaching about and study of test design is necessary. Time spent on applying these skills will help students better analyze test questions they encounter in the future and should have more impact on their learning than isolated mini-lessons on test-taking skills. Alternative uses of student generated questions are limitless. Individual questions can be added to later assessment as review items, or, if submitted on index cards, as game questions. Flash cards, story problems, language translations, etc. could evolve from the student generated questions.

The Answer Is
Provide a list of important concepts or vocabulary words from the unit of study. Have students generate three to four questions that could be answered with the word supplied. If your students have studied Bloom's and Williams' taxonomies, you can designate specific levels/kinds of question you wanted them to use. This method helps students develop skill at predicting what questions might be included on future assessments.

Why Use Performance Assessment?

The creation of quality responses, products, performances, and portfolios:

- supports the conditions identified as being present in brain-compatible learning environments: varied sources of input; active, meaningful learning activities; and timely, appropriate feedback

- requires students to develop literacy as they integrate reading/writing/speaking skills with content knowledge

- promotes student engagement by providing tasks likely to match the multiple intelligences and various styles, aptitudes, and interests of the students

- requires the student to practice, refine, and revise in order to demonstrate learning

- when properly designed, assesses the "essential to know" components of the concepts under study

- gives the student and teacher insights into student thinking, learning-to-learn strategies, and habits

- reflects growth in social and academic skills and behaviors that are not easily demonstrated in paper-and-pencil assessments

- encourages creativity and originality

- promotes the use of processes and information from the world beyond the classroom and school. The tasks are authentic in that they are tasks that people engage in the world beyond academia

- causes school work to be more like the world beyond the classroom through use of the skills and competencies listed in the SCANS report

- demonstrates to the community what students are achieving

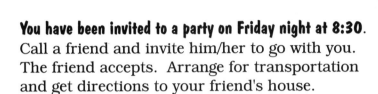

Espanol 1

Examen Final

You have been invited to a party on Friday night at 8:30. Call a friend and invite him/her to go with you. The friend accepts. Arrange for transportation and get directions to your friend's house.

You arrive at the party and greet the host/hostess who warmly welcomes you. You then pay a compliment to him/her.

While there, you get something to eat and discuss your food preferences.

You notice a new boy/girl and ask your host/hostess what his/her name is. You and your friend approach the new girl/boy and introduce yourselves. You ask where he/she is from and where he/she now lives. You talk about the weather and some likes and dislikes (maybe sports, movies, T.V. shows, famous personalities, etc.). You also talk about what school you attend and discuss some courses and teachers. Be sure to express what you think about these things.

You or your friend ask what time it is and announce that you must go home because it is late. You have to study for a Spanish test.

Before leaving, you ask your new friend if he/she would like to go to the movies tomorrow night. Discuss what's playing, what kind of movie it is, and when it begins. Your friend suggests a better movie and you all agree to go.

You then say goodbye to your new friend and the host/hostess.

Characters: **Hostess/Host**
Main Character
Friend
New Boy/Girl

Maureen Mugavin, Worthington Kilbourne High School, Worthington, OH

Espanol 1
Examen Final continued...

Function and Content

Before the party
___ call on phone
___ invite
___ accept an invitation
___ arrange transportation
___ give/get directions (2)

Arrival at the party
___ greet
___ welcome visitor
___ pay a compliment

Party talk
___ food preferences
___ ask name of new person
___ introduce self
___ ask where from
___ ask where lives now
___ talk about weather (2)
___ interest (3)
___ express opinions about courses
    and teachers

Time to go home
___ ask/tell the time
___ announce need to go home
___ announce need to study for a test

Tomorrow's plans
___ ask about movies tomorrow night
___ discuss what movie to see
___ discuss when movie starts
___ suggest a movie
___ agree on a movie
___ say good-bye all around

Required Vocabulary
You must use at least 10 of these words.

Use at least 5 of these verbs in any form.

poder	querer
vivir	creer
asistir	deber
tener que	dar
llamarse	pensar
ir	venir

Use at least 5 of these words.

pelicula
tener ganas de
Que (noun) tan (adjective)
Me gusta (n)
empieza
Por que no?
De donde?
bienvenido
Hace (weather)

See attached rubric for assessment criteria. Note the x6 weighting of functions and content.

Maureen Mugavin, Worthington Kilbourne High School, Worthington, OH

THE USA since WWII
XAP: Still Video Disk
Portfolio

The final assignment of our year is intended to **"capture in pictures"** of the history that has impacted the lives of your grandparents, parents, and yourselves. Form groups of 2 or 3. Each group will be assigned a time period of 4-5 years between 1946 and the present day. The following requirements and optional activities should be included in your portfolio:

1. **Identify 5-8 pictures that are vivid representations of the time period you have been assigned.** They should cover a wide range of topics and represent events/people/issues in the United States and around the world. Once each group has researched the assigned time period and has chosen the events, **the class as a whole will then create a Xap shot portfolio in chronological order.** (50 points)

2. Each group will submit a **detailed description of its pictures**. The "captions" should be typed single-spaced, and thoroughly explain the picture. Where, when, why, who, how, etc., should be answered for each. As your Xap shot is shown on the screen, you will read your information to the class. Be ready to answer any questions AND to explain why you selected the picture. (50 points)

3. Each group is to turn in an **outline map** clearly identifying the location of each picture. Neatness counts! In addition to locating your events, the maps should also include any nearby cities or physical features. The use of color will greatly enhance your finished product and is recommended. (25 points.)

4. Each group is to write a **ONE page summary of your time period**. What was going on in the US? What were the political issues? Which world events influenced US society? How was life changing? etc. Do not merely restate your captions. Go beyond those events and explain the information that is crucial to these years in history. (25 points)

5. **Interview** someone who lived during the years you studied. After introducing them in your opening, ask them which 5 events they most vividly remember. Where were they when they occurred? Why were they important? Did they directly affect their lives? Then, have them critique your choices. Do your pictures correspond with their memories or do they remind them of any forgotten events? (25 points)

Pat Forward, Worthington Kilbourne High School, Worthington, OH

The USA since WWII continued...

Optional: The following could be added to your portfolio or substituted in place of one of the above. Please see me...

6. **Create a musical cassette** that reflects the songs that people listened to during the years you researched. The tape should be 5 minutes in length and will serve as background music while you read your captions.

7. Bring in **artifacts** from your family or friends that represent your time period. Please be careful, however, not to bring items of incredible value.

8. **Write a reflective paper** putting yourself into the years studied and tell whether you would have enjoyed being a teenager "back then." If you have a time period that you actually lived through, what do you think the next 10 years will add to history? Will life become easier, harder, or just different? What could your children's teenage years be like?

9. **Take your own photograph**(s) and show the class an event or issue that you feel will be of impact to your class, school, or community during the next few years. We will add your photos to the end of our class Xap shot.

Years of Research
1946-1950	**1951-1955**	**1956-1960**
1961-1965	**1966-1970**	**1971-1975**
1976-1980	**1981-1985**	**1986-1989**
1990-1993	**1994-1997**	

Remember, as you look for your pictures, **books should not be your only source.** Pictures can be obtained from the Internet, newspapers, and magazines. More recent time periods will require the use of more periodicals. If you are unsure about the clarity of an image, ask me.

Finally, we will spend 2-3 days in the computer lab typing your written work. At the same time, some of you may still access the library or find a quiet place to complete your maps. Your project will be graded based on the attached rubric and will include a self-evaluation and a critique of how well your group cooperated with each other. Please create a folder to put your portfolio pieces into and be prepared to present your research during the exam period.

Total Points = 175

Pat Forward, Worthington Kilbourne High School, Worthington, OH

What is a Rubric?

A rubric is a set of criteria, expressed as a scale, used to assess levels of student performance.

Rubrics:

- Specify how student work is to be assessed

- list and explicitly describe behaviors, processes or products that can be observed

- include precise criteria so there is little inference or subjective judgment

- once designed, require far less teacher time for critiquing student products and assigning ratings

- make expectations clear and assessment seem equitable to students and parents

- are given to students as the assignment or performance task is introduced

- allow students to monitor how they are progressing and to make necessary corrections along the way

- can be either holistic or analytical in form; analytical rubrics are best used with formative assessment while holistic rubrics are often used with summative assessments

- Rubrics are most effective in promoting student success when they are used in conjunction with models or exemplars of student work. Models should be developmentally appropriate yet vary in meeting the criteria. With older students, a professional model can also be included. Students learn to use the rubric to analyze the models, and, therefore, become even clearer about the requirements of the task before they begin work.

Creating a Rubric

The process of creating rubrics is an ongoing one. If you do not have examples of student work at various levels of performance, the descriptions may, at first, be more quantitative than qualitative. When possible gather student work samples for your own use as well as for exemplars for students; if that is not possible the first time you used the task with the rubric, you might complete a product and analyze the component parts to complete the rubric.

Score Description

5 Work is beyond expectations. The quality of the work is unusually high.

4 Work meets developmentally appropriate expectations. The work demonstrates that the student can apply the skill and/or knowledge in this task.

3 Work is almost completed to the described standard. There are minor problems, errors, or omissions.

2 The work is presented and the skills and/or knowledge is evident in some ways, but there are major flaws, errors, or omissions.

1 The skills/knowledge is not demonstrated.

♦ Experienced rubric designers suggest that when creating a five level rubric, start with the "meets expectations" descriptors on the fourth level. You can ask yourself:

What are my expectations or specific goals for this task?

What behaviors will a student who has mastered the skill display?

What level of performance do I hope all students will attain?

After that it is natural to move to "exceeds" and "does not meet" descriptors.

RUBRIC for WRITING ASSESSMENT
in a foreign language

5   **Demonstrates High Proficiency**
-Well organized; ideas presented clearly and logically
-Few grammatical or spelling errors
-Wide variety of grammar, vocabulary, and sentence structures
-Few word-order errors
-Writing is appropriate to current level
-Thorough response to the question

4   **Clearly Demonstrates Proficiency**
-Loosely organized, but main ideas present
-Some grammatical or spelling errors
-Some variety of grammar, vocabulary, and sentence structures
-Some word-order errors
-Most of the writing is appropriate to current level
-Generally thorough response to the question

3   **Demonstrates Progress Toward Proficiency**
-Some attempts at organization, but with confused sequencing
-Many word-order errors
-Writing is below current level
-Partial response to the question

2   **Demonstrates Strong Need for Intervention**
-Lack of organization
-Significant and serious grammatical and spelling errors
-Lack of variety of grammar, vocabulary, and sentence structure
-Excessive word-order errors
-Writing is well below current level
-Insufficient response to the question

1   **Unacceptable**
-Response falls below the above descriptions or is inappropriate

adapted from Ohio State Department of Education

Colonial Brochure Rubric

Holistic Rubric Example

4

"We Can't Keep 'Em Away"
This brochure is truly exceptional in every way; it is sure to cause a steady stream of settlers to your colony!
Work shows evidence of outside research including technology.
Colony name is identified.
Colony founder is identified.
Map of where colony is found is labeled, colored, and includes a key.
Descriptions of political, economic, and social interests are supported by facts and details.
Complete sentences and paragraphing are used and contain no mistakes.
Brochure is neatly typed or written in ink.
Brochure is colorful and includes illustrations with explicit captions.

3

"Lots of Interest"
This brochure is right on target and will cause many curious travelers to come to call!
It meets all requirements or exceeds them.
The brochure shows evidence of outside research.
Colony name is identified.
Colony founder is identified.
Map of where colony is found is labeled, colored, and includes a key.
Description of political, economic, and social interests are mostly supported with facts and details.
Complete sentences and paragraphing are mostly used.
Brochure is neatly typed or written in ink.
Brochure is colorful and includes illustrations.

2

"Occasional Traveler"
This brochure may go to the bottom of the stack. You may get the occasional traveler to your colony.
The colony name is identified.
The founder is identified.
Map of where colony is found is labeled, colored, and includes a key.
Description of political, economic, and social interests are included but need some supportive details.
Complete sentences and paragraphing are used; there are however, errors in form.
The brochure is colorful, but lacks informative illustrations.
The brochure is generally neat and is typed or written in ink with some errors.

1

"The Desperate Searcher"
This brochure is incomplete, but may attract the desperate colonist!
Colony name is identified.
Colony founder is identified.
Map of where colony is found is included but may be lacking in labels, color, a key.
Description of political, economic, and social interests are lacking detail.
The use of complete sentences and paragraphing need revision.
Brochure hard to read with smudges and wrinkles.

Suzanne Blue, Rush-Henrietta Central School District, NY

Bedroom Cleaning Rubric*

Analytical Rubric Example

Bed

5 + Bed is made with no wrinkles, looks neat and inviting.
+ Bottom and corners of sheets and blankets tucked in.
+ pillows are centered at one end of bed.

3 + Bed is made with some wrinkles, covers pulled up but not neatly.
+ Bottom and Corners not tucked in.
+ Pillows uncentered or thrown onto bed carelessly.

1 + Bed is not made or covers just thrown onto mattress.

Floor

5 + No toys, clothes, papers, etc., on floor.
+ Floor is clean and vacuumed, even in corners.
+ Under the bed is clean.

3 + No toys, clothes, papers, etc. on floor.
+ Floor has not been vacuumed.
+ Under the bed is clean.

1 + Objects are out-of-place and on floor.
+ Floor is not clean or vacuumed.
+ Objects "hiding" under bed.

Closet

5 + The closet is neat overall, clothes are hung up in appropriate places.
+ Dirty clothes are in the laundry hamper.
+ Toys, blocks, games, and other objects are put away neatly.

3 + Clothes are hung up, but look messy or are misplaced.
+ Some objects scattered on floor or put away incorrectly.

1 + Both dirty and clean clothes are on the floor.
+ Toys and other objects look as if they were thrown in.

Total Bedroom Cleaning Score:

_____ out of _____ **15**

*Original source unknown.
This rubric is part of the folklore of our profession.

©Just ASK Publications, ASK Inc.

163

Collaborative Chamber Music Unit: An Integrated Unit of Music and Guidance

Exemplary	Competent	Novice	No Attempt
makes independent, intelligent fingering decisions in order to meet the technical and musical demands of the piece	needs occasional prompts for fingering	requires all fingering to be noted	even with written in fingerings, cannot accomplish
employs standard bowing rules and knows when they do not apply. Works with other students to make bowing coordinate between individual parts	demonstrates knowledge of bowing rules but cannot make adjustments when required	begins the piece with proper direction, but frequently gets lost	randomly bows
reads and performs written rhythms, tonal patterns, bowings where applicable and symbols and instructions in the music	starts and stops together, plays together but lacks artistic component	knows only segments of the music; group performance lacks rhythmic constancy	does not know music, therefore, group cannot perform
adjusts intonation independently and in relation to the rest of group	adjusts intonation independently but does not adjust in relation to the rest of group	demonstrates a basis of tonality but consistently plays out of tune. Does not adjust to rest of group.	fails to demonstrate an understanding of tonality
demonstrates technical and creative ability to plan and lead a productive rehearsal using a simple score; anticipates problem area and has a plan for solving them	plans and leads a rehearsal; anticipates problem areas	demonstrates the ability to lead a rehearsal	makes no attempt to lead a rehearsal
demonstrates personal responsibility by having a written plan with 3 to 5 objectives, and four or five ways to accomplish each objective	has a written plan for each rehearsal student is to run and two methods of accomplishing each objective	has a written plan with a simple goal but little idea of how to get there	does not have a plan and does not run the group
listens to other's ideas; synthesizes the group's ideas; works to facilitate exchange of ideas; brings new ideas forward to the group; recognizes and advocates good ideas; facilitates the trying of a variety of approaches to the music	listens to others; presents some of own ideas but gives up easily when ideas not accepted; advocates for self; does not advocate for others; does not hinder group process but does not always work to move it forward	does not independently put forth ideas, but willingly follows the group	does not contribute any ideas and hinders the group process

Laurie Kennedy and Willie Buchholz, Irodequoit High School, Rochester, NY

Performance Task Lists

A performance task assessment list provides an alternative to the rubric. This assessment tool resembles the lists many of us have used to assess student projects or papers **after the students turn in their work.** We have often attached the criteria to the paper as we returned it so that students can better understand how we determined the grade we assigned the work. This task list, however, has several important characteristics not included in the lists we have used in the past...especially giving the students the criteria and point values **before they begin work**. Educators in Pomerang Regional School District 15 in Connecticut have worked collaboratively to develop this assessment tool, which they consider a critical part of performance-based learning and assessment.

Steps in the Development of Performance Task Assessment Lists

▶Identify the **standard** focus and determine clearly what students are to know and be able to do as a result of the unit of study.

▶Design student **tasks that focus** on the **content knowledge** needed to demonstrate mastery and on the **process skills** and **work habits** students need in order to be successful.

▶Do a **task analysis** both during and following task design.

▶Make a **list of the components** of the performance task.

▶**Assign points to each component** to match the significance of the component and the areas of need of the student(s).

▶Provide/create **models** of work (both acceptable and unacceptable).

When using performance task lists with **primary students,** the ratings may be "terrific," "okay," and "needs work." The educators in Connecticut recommend pictures such as smiling and frowning faces for an age appropriate rating scale. As the students mature, both the components and the ratings become more complex.

One of the powerful aspects of performance task lists is that they can be used to **differentiate instruction** by simply changing the components listed on the task list or by adjusting the number of points assigned to a specific component.

Chemistry Mini-Lectures
Energy & Disorder /Reaction Rate

GUIDELINES:

1. You will be working in a group of 3 or 4 to develop a mini-lesson on one of the following topics:

> **Enthalpy and Entropy**
> **Free Energy and Standard States**
> **Reversible Reactions and Reaction Rate**
> **Nature of Reactants and Concentration**
> **Temperature and Catalysis**
> **Reaction Mechanism**

2. All group members should be involved in the preparation and presentation. The presentation should be approximately 15 minutes long and include components listed below.

3. Your work will be scored for its efforts and the resulting product according to the points assigned to each component.

4. You will view videotapes of previous presentations as models to evaluate.

5. The assessment of this material will be derived from the contents of the six group assessments. You may use any presentation notes and handouts on the test.

COMPONENTS:

	Possible Points	Self Assessment	Teacher Assessment
Attention Grabber	5		
Supplemental Information (topic expanded beyond textbook)	5		
Transparencies or Handouts	5		
Visual Aids (poster, laser disk, pictures, model, etc.)	10		
Demonstration/Lecture	25		
Active Learning Strategies to Engage Class in the Topic	15		
Checks for Understanding (questions, problem, etc.)	15		
Assessment (5 questions typed with answer sheet)	20		
TOTAL POINTS	100		

Renee DeWald, Evanston Township High School, Evanston, IL

You could select from, and perhaps add to, this list of components for a research paper to design a performance task list. The selected variables, number of variables, the points assigned to a variable, and the language used would vary with the age of the student and the areas of focus.

Performance Task List for a Research Report

	Possible Points	Self Assessment	Teacher Assessment

1. The thesis statement clearly defines topic and purpose.

2. The introduction captures the reader's attention by explaining the significance of the topic.

3. The body of the paper is composed of paragraphs that divide the topic and contain ideas supported by appropriate details.

4. Transitions between ideas and paragraphs are smooth.

5. Information is accurate, effectively used, arranged in a logical order, and is sufficient to support the thesis.

6. Information sources are relevant and relate to the thesis. Sources are cited, then listed in bibliography.

8. The paper provides evidence of age-appropriate quality thinking about the topic.

9. The conclusion has a reminder of the thesis statement, summarizes the main points, and creates a sense of closure.

10. The paper is concise.

11. The paper is free of spelling errors, follows the rules for punctuation and capitalization, and uses abbreviations appropriately.

12. Any graphics add to, rather than detract from, the clarity of the paper and include information important to the report.

13. The bibliography follows the identified format.

14. Spacing and formatting, including title page, heading, subheadings, footnotes, and margins, are correctly done.

15. Grammar, sentence structure, and word selection follow conventions of standard written English.

16. The paper is typed neatly and is presented in an appropriate font type and size.

Terry Furgason and Brent Comer, Jennings County High School, North Vernon, IN

What is a Portfolio?

A portfolio is a collection of student work, in draft and/or completed form, which represents students' efforts, progress and achievements. The critical attribute that distinguishes a portfolio from a scrapbook is student reflection on the work and on their learning, their struggles, and their growth over time.

Decisions that have to be made by teacher and students when planning to use portfolios as a part of assessment include:

➢What will be placed in the portfolios?

➢What criteria/procedures will be used to place items in the portfolio?

➢What process will be used for providing feedback?

➢What process will be used to facilitate student reflection and self assessment?

➢What factors, including the criteria and standards, will be used to assess the portfolio

➢Who will evaluate the portfolio?

➢Is there an audience other than the student and the teacher?

➢What kind of binder or containers will be used?

➢How will the contents be arranged?

Teachers and students work together to plan, compile, and organize contents, and assess the portfolio. The age and the skills of the learner, the course of study, and the purposes of the portfolio determine the appropriate degree of teacher guidance.

Why Use Portfolios?

The portfolio process provides an opportunity for assessment of learning and accomplishments *over time* and for assessment, not only of *mastery* of identified *standards and objectives,* but of the *process of learning* as well. Additionally, the portfolio process permits the assessment of a *broader range of thinking skills* than can be accomplished with more traditional paper and pencil assessments. Students are able to assess the *effectiveness of their own efforts* and, over time, become more independent as learners.

Possible Criteria
for Assessing Portfolios

accuracy of information
peer editing
evidence of growth from errors
completeness
connections to other subjects
development of process
diversity of selections
evidence of collaboration
following directions
growth and development
insightfulness
evidence of critical thinking
knowledge of content
mechanics, usage, grammar
organization suitable to purpose
originality / creativity
persistence / revisions
personal expression
reflections
error analysis
responses to conference questions
self-assessment
timeliness
use of multiple intelligences
variety of entries
visual appeal

♦ **Each item in the portfolio does not have to be graded. The overall portfolio can be graded on the basis of specific criteria.**

♦ **Teacher and/or students choose specific variables to assess.**

♦ **Any component can be weighted to reflect importance in relation to standards of learning or to reflect the skills on which a particular student is working.**

Group and Self Assessment

Use a separate piece of paper to respond to these questions. Please write your responses in complete sentences.

1. What did **you** do to **contribute** to the success of your presentation? **Be specific.**

2. List the names of your **group's members** and tell about their **contributions** to the success of your presentation.

3. What did you **learn about yourself** from doing this presentation?

4. What did you **learn about your group members** from doing this presentation?

5. What did you **learn about your topic** from doing this presentation?

6. What did you **learn about your community** and the available resources?

7. What grade would you give **yourself** for **your effort in the research and presentation** of your topic?

8. List the names of your **group's members** and give each of them a **grade for their effort** in the research and presentation of your topic.

9. What did you like **most** and **least** about your presentation?

10. Do you have any **other comments** you would like to express regarding this presentation?

Dan Struck, Jennings County High School, North Vernon, IN

Individual Participation Rating Sheet

First, rate yourself in each area. Then have each of your teammates rate your participation. If they agree with your self assessment, they need only initial the rating you recorded. If any teammate disagrees, that teammate should record the score and present the rationale on the back of this rating sheet.

	Almost Always	Often	Sometimes	Rarely
	3	2	1	0
TEAM PARTICIPATION				
Participated in discussions				
Did fair share of work				
Allowed others to work				
GROUP PROCESS				
Helped plan how to accomplish task				
Helped identify and solve problems				
Summarized and clarified				
Praised efforts of others				
Compromised and worked for consensus				
RESPONSIBILITY				
Came to class on time				
Came to class with materials				
Did what I said I would do				

John Banker, Rush-Henrietta High School, Henrietta, NY

Products
&
Perspectives

TOP TEN QUESTIONS
to ask myself as I design lessons

1. What should **students know and be able to do** with what they know as a result of this lesson? How are these objectives related to national, state, and/or district standards or proficiencies?

2. How will students demonstrate what they know and what they can do with what they know? What will be the assessment criteria and what form will it take?

3. How will **I find out** what **students already know,** and how will I help them access what they know and have experienced both inside and outside the classroom? How will **I help them** not only **build on prior experiences**, but **deal with misconceptions** and reframe their thinking when appropriate?

4. How will new knowledge, concepts, and skills be introduced? Given the diversity of my students, what are **my best options for sources and presentation modes** of new material?

5. How will I facilitate student processing (meaning making) of new information or processes? What are the key questions, activities, and assignments (in class or homework)?

6. How will **I check for student understanding** during the lesson?

7. What do I need to do to **differentiate instruction** so that the learning experiences are productive for all students?

8. How will I **"Frame the Learning"** so that **students know the objectives**, the **rationale** for the objectives and activities, the directions and procedures, as well as the **assessment criteria** at the beginning of the learning process?

9. How will I build in opportunities for students to make real world connections and to learn and use the varied and complex thinking skills they need to succeed in the classroom and the world beyond?

10. What adjustments need to be made in the **learning environment** so that we can work and learn efficiently during this study?

Potential Products

A

action plan
album
annotated bibliography
area graph
autobiography
adventure

advertisement
anagram
apparatus
artifact collection
anecdote

advice column
animation
aquarium
audiotape recording
application

B

ballad
bar graph
block picture story
book report
brainteaser
bulletin board
book

ballet
bio-poem
blueprint
booklet
brochure
business letter

banner
bill of rights
book jacket
bookmark
bullet chart
biographical sketch

C

calendar
cartoon
ceramics
characterization
cinquin
clothing
column chart
commercial
conference presentation
costume
critique
conversation
case study

campaign speech
CD cover
charade
checklist
classification list/system
collage
comedy act
comparison
constitution
couplet
crossword puzzle
children's book

cardboard relief
celebrity profile
chart
choral reading
classified ad
collection
comic book
computer program
conversation
coupon
caption
commentary

Potential Products continued...

D

dance	database	debate
demonstration	description	diagram
dialogue	diary	dictionary
diorama	display	display case
documentary	dramatization	drawing
directions		

E

editorial	editorial cartoon	equipment
essay	estimate	etching
exaggeration	experiment	explanation
error analysis	eyewitness account	

F

fabric design	fairy tale	field manual
field trip	filmstrip	finger puppets
flag	flannel board	flash cards
flip charts	flow chart	food
free verse	friendly letter	furniture

G

gadget	gallery	game
gauge	glossary	gossip column
graph	graphic organizer	greeting card
guidebook	goal	

Potential Products continued...

H

haiku	hand puppet	handbook
handout	hat	headline
hieroglyphic	history	hologram
hypothesis		

I

icon	identification cards	illustration
imprint	index	interview
interview script	invitation	interpretive dance
inquiry	invention	

J

jigsaw puzzle	jingle	job description
joke	joke book	journal
journal article		

K

kit	kitchen tool	kite

L

law	lawyer's brief	layout
learning center	lecture	lesson plan
letter	letter of request	letter to the editor
letter of complaint	letter of support	limerick
list	lithograph	log
logic puzzle	lyrics	lab report

Potential Products continued...

M

machine	macramé	map
marionette	mask	memorandum
metaphor	meter	mime
mnemonic	mobile	model
monologue	monument	mosaic
movement game	mural	music
musical composition	musical instrument	myth
montage	matrix	monograph
	manual	

N

newscast	newsletter	newspaper
newspaper ad	newspaper article	novel
nursery rhyme	notes	

O

oath	observation sheet	oral report
origami	order form	outline
operator's manual	owner's manual	

P

painting	pamphlet	parody
patent	pattern	pen pal letter
pennant	petition	photo essay
photograph	pictograph	picture dictionary
pie chart	plan	plane
planet description	play	playing cards
poem	poster	prediction
profile	proposal	prototype
puppet show	puzzle	prophecy

Potential Products continued...

Q

quatrain	quarterly report	questionnaire
question	quilt	

R

radio announcement	radio commentary	radio commercial
rap	rationale	recipe
report	reproduction	research report
review	rewrite	rewritten ending
rhyme	riddle	role-play
rubric	request	reply
resume	response	rebuttal

S

satire	scenario	schedule
science fiction story	scrapbook	scroll
sewing project	short story	skit
ship	ship's log	sign
silk screen	slide show	slogan
soap opera	song	speech
stencil	stick puppet	story
story problem	survey	symbol
solution	sculpture	script
simulation		

T

tall tale	taxonomy	telegram
television newscast	television sitcom	time line
transparency	travel advertisement	travel log
textbook	theory	3-D display
toy	translation	thumbnail sketch
task analysis		

Potential Products continued...

U

UFO understudy underwater scene
utopia

V

verdict verification videotape
video yearbook visual aid vocabulary list
voice-over Venn diagram

W

wall hanging wanted poster warm-up
warrant for arrest warranty wax sculpture
weather map web window shade
writing word game web page
word search

X

x-ray xylophone

Y

yardstick year-in-review yearbook

Z

zodiac chart zoo guidebook

Potential Perspectives

A

artist
architect
actor/actress
author
astronaut
aviator
alien
actuary
admiral

atheist
archaeologist
anthropologist
animator
astronomer
astrologer
acrobat
aborigine
accountant

acquaintance
administrator
aunt
ambassador
academy award
    nominee
ambulance driver
activist

B

baby
brother
basketball player
baseball player
baker
boat captain
ballet dancer

bullfighter
boss
bully
baby-sitter
butcher
blackjack dealer
bartender

boxer
bellhop
bandleader
boy
bandit
beautician

C

computer programmer
cyclist
comedian
composer
cop
custodian
carpenter
college student
calligrapher

counselor
crossing guard
chicken farmer
cat breeder
chef
cartoonist
cosmetologist
coach
clown

criminal
convict
candidate
Congressperson
chairperson
committee member
comic strip character
captain

Potential Perspectives continued...

D

doctor	drummer	decorator
director	dad	dentist
dish washer	derelict	diver
dancer	dog trainer	delegate
disc jockey	drug dealer	democrat
dictator	daredevil	dermatologist

E

editor	equestrian	emir
executive	exterminator	emperor
environmentalist	educator	enemy
electrician	elephant trainer	engineer
EMT	economist	educator

F

firefighter	fitness expert	flight attendant
forest ranger	fairy	furrier
football player	father	facilitator
fisherman	female	fictional character
friend	ferryman	falconer
farmer	financier	fashion designer

G

gardener	general	geologist
governor	gambler	ghost
giant	game warden	grocer
gymnast	garbage collector	government official
grandparent	gangster	

Potential Perspectives continued...

H

hair stylist	housekeeper	heart surgeon
high jumper	hula dancer	housewife
hero/heroine	hippie	historical figure
historian	hang glider	hunchback
hunter	halfback	harlequin

I

ice skater	iconographer	illusionist
ice cream man	idealist	illustrator
ichthyologist	idiot	immortal

J

juror	jazz singer	journalist
judge	jester	justice of the peace
janitor	jockey	juvenile
jeweler	juggler	

K

karate instructor	keyboardist	kickboxer
kid	kindergartener	kayaker
kleptomaniac	king	khan

L

logger	life guard	lady
lawyer	librarian	lecturer

Potential Perspectives continued...

M

mail carrier	musician	magician
Maytag repair man	mayor	member of...
military officer	mountain climber	moderate
mother	machinist	monster
marriage counselor	mafioso	maid

N

nurse	numerologist	nomad
neighbor	nanny	nuclear physicist
newspaper carrier	nephew/niece	novice
night watchman	neurologist	navigator
nun	news anchor	Nazi
newsanchor	newlywed	naval officer

O

optometrist	ornithologist	observer
operator	opera singer	officer
orator	official	Olympian

P

president	painter	pagan
parent	psychologist	palm reader
principal	piano tuner	preacher
producer	pianist	patron
photographer	paleontologist	patriarch
psychiatrist	publisher	pauper
police officer	puppeteer	peon
professor	pirate	politician
pilot	psychic	poet
paratrooper	pacifist	participant

Potential Perspectives continued...

realtor	runner	referee
reverend	rugby player	refugee
rabbi	Rastafarian	relative
race car driver	rock star	republican
reporter	rebel	radiologist
researcher	receptionist	radical

sister	superhero	scholar
secretary	stewardess	schoolteacher
senator	scientist	sailor
student	sculptor	soldier
senior citizen	security guard	second baseman
soccer player	singer	school board member
seeing eye dog	stuntman	superintendent
surgeon	sales clerk	salesperson
seamstress	scapegoat	saint

T

truck driver	taxi driver	transient
tourist	tax collector	translator
tour guide	technician	traveler
travel agent	tenant	trespasser
teacher	terrorist	troll
toddler	therapist	troubadour
tap dancer	ticket agent	troublemaker
tyrant	townspeople	tutor
tennis player	traitor	typist
tailor	tradesman	television star

Potential Perspectives continued...

U

uncle	umpire	urbanite
urologist	union member	urchin
understudy	unicyclist	usher

V

veteran	vampire	villian
veterinarian	vagabond	vegetarian
vandal	vagrant	ventriloquist

W

writer	worker	warden
witch	waif	wrestler
waitress/waiter	wallflower	weightlifter

X

X-ray technician	xylophonist	xenophobe

Y

yachtsman	yeoman	yodeler
Yankee	yuppie	yogi

Z

zookeeper	zealot	zombie

LET'S GO RAFTING!

Identify a concept, topic, or event your students are studying, use (or have the students use) the choices listed in Potential Products and Potential Perspectives lists and it's RAFTS AWAY!
See pages 129-133 for examples.

Role _____
Audience _____
Form (product) _____
Time _____

Role _____
Audience _____
Form (product) _____
Time _____

Role _____
Audience _____
Form (product) _____
Time _____

Differentiation
of
Instruction

One size doesn't fit all!

VIII

TOP TEN QUESTIONS
to ask myself as I design lessons

1. What should **students know and be able to do** with what they know as a result of this lesson? How are these objectives related to national, state, and/or district standards or proficiencies?

2. How will **students demonstrate what they know and what they can do** with what they know? What will be the **assessment criteria** and what form will it take?

3. How will **I find out** what **students already know,** and how will I help them access what they know and have experienced both inside and outside the classroom? How will **I help them** not only **build on prior experiences,** but **deal with misconceptions** and **reframe their thinking** when appropriate?

4. How will new knowledge, concepts, and skills be introduced? Given the diversity of my students, what are **my best options for sources and presentation modes** of new material?

5. How will **I facilitate student processing (meaning making)** of new information or processes? What are the key questions, activities, and assignments (in class or homework)?

6. How will **I check for student understanding** during the lesson?

7. **What do I need to do to differentiate instruction so that the learning experiences are productive for all students?**

8. How will I **"Frame the Learning"** so that **students know the objectives,** the **rationale** for the objectives and activities, the directions and procedures, as well as the **assessment criteria** at the beginning of the learning process?

9. How will I build in opportunities for students to make **real world connections** and to learn and use the **varied and complex thinking skills** they need to succeed in the classroom and the world beyond?

10. **What adjustments need to be made in the learning environment so that we can work and learn efficiently during this study?**

Successful Learners...

- are motivated to learn and set learning goals
- think about what they know
- take responsibility for their own learning
- anticipate what they are to learn
- participate actively in their classes
- assimilate, consolidate and integrate new knowledge
- are organized and try to manage their time well
- are persistent and are effective problem solvers
- seek comprehension and meaning
- monitor their own learning
- construct meaning

Struggling Learners...

- ✗ are easily distracted
- ✗ tend to have short attention spans
- ✗ lack self-confidence
- ✗ demonstrate inappropriate communication and interpersonal skills
- ✗ have difficulty demonstrating empathy for others
- ✗ often have limited experience bases and range of interests
- ✗ do not know how to analyze the effectiveness of their efforts
- ✗ do not see cause and effect relationships
- ✗ appear not to learn from previous mistakes or errors in judgment
- ✗ avoid failure by avoiding tasks
- ✗ lack organizational skills
- ✗ appear to avoid responsibility

Inclusive Instruction

Teaching Advanced Learners

1. Discover and acknowledge what they already know.

2. Provide a balance of skill building and meaning making activities.

3. Plan and guide them in planning projects that capitalize on their interests.

4. Allow them some flexibility in the way they use their time.

5. Allow them to learn at a different pace than their peers.

6. Plan a variety of reality based learning experiences; both teacher and students monitor the effectiveness.

7. Help them to be aware of and use productive learning strategies.

8. Teach them to be self-sufficient; only do for them as much as you need to do.

9. Encourage them to demonstrate mastery in a wide variety of ways.

Teaching Struggling Learners

1. Discover and acknowledge what they already know.

2. Provide a balance of skill building and meaning making activities.

3. Plan and guide them in planning projects that capitalize on their interests.

4. Allow them some flexibility in the way they use their time.

5. Allow them to learn at a different pace than their peers.

6. Plan a variety of reality based learning experiences; both teacher and students monitor the effectiveness.

7. Help them to be aware of and use productive learning strategies.

8. Teach them to be self-sufficient; only do for them as much as you need to do.

9. Encourage them to demonstrate mastery in a wide variety of ways.

Adapted from Susan Winebrenner: *Teaching Gifted Kids in the Regular Classroom*, Free Spirit Publishing, 1992

Task Analysis

Task analysis: (*noun*) The systematic breakdown of the tasks we ask students to complete. Task analysis allows us to identify the skills, both academic and process, that the students need in order to successfully complete the task, assignment, or project.

How To Analyze a Task

● Make sure the task is worth doing.

● Note and list all the **components** that go into accomplishing the task.

● Note and list all the **skills (procedural knowledge)** and bits of **declarative knowledge** students need to have in order to be successful with the task.

● Identify the levels of understanding they will need to complete the task.

● Use **cognitive empathy** to check through the task one more time. Better yet, if this is a high stakes assignment, have someone not in a your class (student, teacher, or friend) read through the task and the directions to check for possible problem areas.

● Identify **which students have mastered which skills.** If unknown, decide how to find out or how to circumvent the need for the skill.

● **Design your instruction** by deciding what to do about the skills or knowledge the entire group needs and what to do about those students who lack the prerequisite skills to be successful even with the beginning components of the task. While there will no doubt be many skill sets and chunks of knowledge you will plan as learning experiences for the entire class, you may choose to organize **mini lessons** to teach focus groups needed skills, have **students teach each other** the problematic skills, or **provide the information** students will need to complete this part of the task. **Prevention of problems** or failure, rather than intervention later, will make you and your students **more successful**. In the end, it will save time and energy for all involved.

The ultimate goal is for our students to do a task analysis independently. This is not only a school skill, but a life skill as well.

Task Analysis

Assignment/Task

_____

Skills and Knowledge Embedded in Task

1._____ 6._____
2._____ 7._____
3._____ 8._____
4._____ 9._____
5._____ 10._____

Is there background knowledge or a level of understanding the entire group is lacking? How about individual students?

Are there skills the entire group is lacking? How about the skill level of individuals?

What shall I do in a proactive way to prevent frustrations and problems with learning?

Students	Potential Problem	Possible Intervention

Principles of Differentiation

1. Learning and assessment for all students is focused on **essential to know concepts and skills** as identified in state and district standards.

2. Learning experiences and types and degree of teacher support are selected based on a **task analysis** that includes an analysis of the skills and knowledge embedded in the task, plus an analysis of **student readiness/background knowledge levels**, **interests**, and **information processing styles.**

3. **Sources of information** are provided at various reading levels, in different languages, and in varying formats to match the needs of learners.

4. **All students** are engaged in **meaningful tasks** that provide balance between skill building and meaning making.

5. The **teacher** is **knowledgeable about content** to be taught, is skilled at **basics of pedagogy**, and the **orchestration of productive learning environments** and can, therefore, concentrate on the needs of the learners.

6. There is a balance between **student** and **teacher choice** of working conditions, sources of information, methods of processing learning, and demonstrating that learning.

7. **Grouping of students is flexible** in that students work individually, in small groups, and in whole class settings. Grouping is based on a variety of factors, including readiness levels and interests.

8. Students are given **precise, public,** and **prior guidelines for performance** tasks and assessments; **models** or exemplars accompany the guidelines.

9. The teacher **collaborates with colleagues** and is **reflective about the impact of instructional decisions** so as to make informed decisions about organizational and instructional strategies.

10. **Learning is the constant; time and teacher support are the variables.**

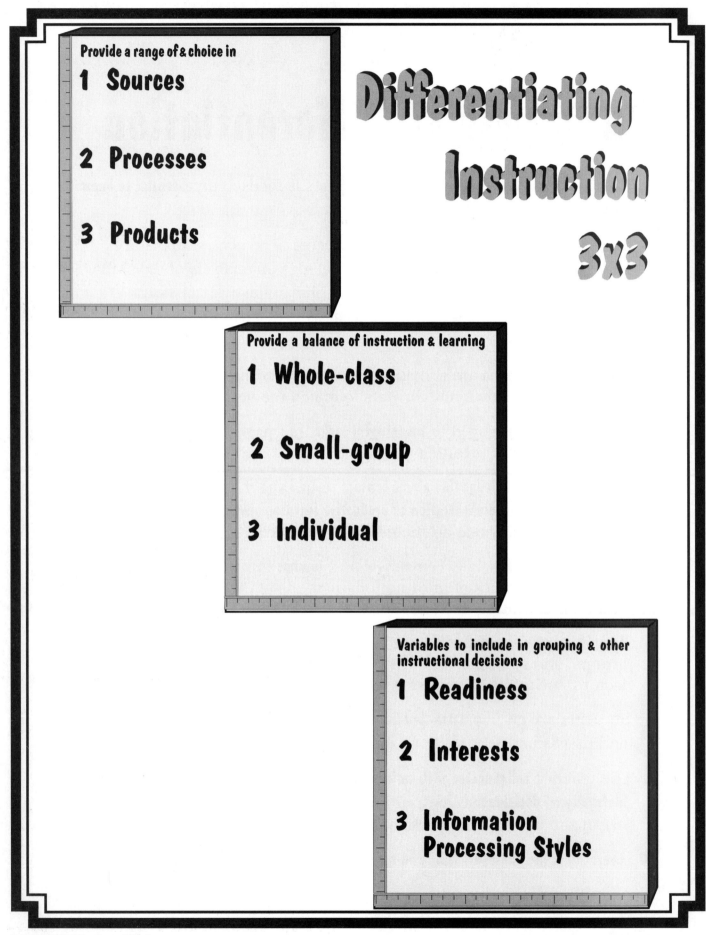

Differentiating Instruction 3x3

Provide a range of & choice in

1 Sources

2 Processes

3 Products

Provide a balance of instruction & learning

1 Whole-class

2 Small-group

3 Individual

Variables to include in grouping & other instructional decisions

1 Readiness

2 Interests

3 Information Processing Styles

Variables to Consider for Differentiation of Instruction & Assessment

The unwavering constant is student engagement in meaningful and rigorous learning experiences. Thoughtful adjustment of these variables can help students move toward competency with the identified standards without "watering down" the material to be mastered.

Grouping Practices

Degree of Independence in Work and Decision Making

Complexity & Challenge of Process and Product

Variety and Range of Materials and Resources

Task Analysis

Pace of Learning and Production

Use of Assessment Results to Inform Teaching and Learning

Individual, Small, and Large Group Instruction and Work

Student Choice

Formats for Processing and Demonstrating Learning

Frequency and Degree of Teacher Support

Various Kinds of Readiness... Reading, Math, and Beyond!

Learning and Information Processing Styles

Reaching More Students
through
Visual, Auditory, & Kinesthetic Modalities

To Emphasize VISUAL Learning . . .

📖 Write directions on the chalkboard, as well as giving them verbally. Give a copy of assignments in written form, weekly or daily.

📖 Use flash cards printed in bold colors.

📖 Supplement lectures with colorful transparencies shown on the overhead projector. Also use models, charts, graphs, and other visual aids.

📖 Allow students to read assignments rather than depending on oral presentations.

📖 Use and teach students to use graphic organizers.

📖 Have students take notes on important words, concepts, or ideas.

📖 Provide a written copy of board work if student has difficulty copying.

To Emphasize AUDITORY Learning . . .

🔔 Record assignment directions on tape or cassette so that the student can replay them as needed.

🔔 Give verbal as well as written directions.

🔔 Tape textbook materials for the student to listen to while reading. Tape only the most important information and simplify or explain the vocabulary.

🔔 Give an oral rather than written test or allow tests to be administered by the special education teacher in the resource room.

🔔 If practice is needed, student can use tape recorder to recite and then play back. A student can practice aloud with another student.

🔔 Substitute oral reports or other written projects for written assignments.

🔔 Have another student read important information to the student.

To Emphasize KINESTHETIC or TACTILE Learning . . .

✋ Use frequent classroom demonstration and participatory modeling.

✋ Allow student to build models, draw pictures, make a display or a video, do an experiment, or give a dramatization.

✋ Use role-play and simulations.

✋ Provide a lecture outline for the student and give note taking instructions.

✋ Allow the student to move about, for example, to another seating area during class.

✋ Use manipulative objects, especially when teaching abstract concepts, such as fractional parts, measurement, and geometry.

Reaching More Students
through
Analytical & Global Learning Preferences

ANALYTICAL thinkers tend to prefer to think and work in these ways.

- ○ process through intellectual lens
- ○ structured/planned
- ○ control feelings
- ○ sequential
- ○ logical
- ○ remember names
- ○ rational
- ○ solve problems by breaking them apart
- ○ time-oriented
- ○ auditory/visual learner
- ○ prefer to write & talk
- ○ follow spoken directions
- ○ prefer T/F, multiple choice, matching
- ○ take fewer risks
- ○ look for differences
- ○ think mathematically
- ○ think of one thing at a time
- ○ judge objectively

GLOBAL thinkers tend to prefer to think and work in these ways.

- ○ process intuitively
- ○ spontaneous
- ○ let feelings go
- ○ creative/responsive
- ○ more abstract
- ○ remember faces
- ○ more likely to act on emotions
- ○ solve problems by looking at whole
- ○ spatially oriented
- ○ kinesthetic learners
- ○ prefer to draw & handle objects
- ○ follow written or demonstrated directions
- ○ talk to think and learn
- ○ "picture" things to think & learn
- ○ prefer essay tests
- ○ take more risks
- ○ look for similar qualities
- ○ think simultaneously

Three Key Points

Provide learners with opportunities to work in their "comfort zone" and opportunities to stretch their thinking and develop skills at working in ways that are not as natural for them.

To help students maximize efforts be aware of which students are comfortable/uncomfortable with the tasks they are doing.

We have a tendency to ask students to work and think in ways that are comfortable or productive for us so it requires careful planning to include learning experiences for all learning preferences.

How I'll Show What I Know

To demonstrate what I have learned about _____ I want to:

_____write a report   _____do a photo essay

_____compile a scrapbook   _____build a model

_____put on a demonstration   _____do a statistical chart

_____set up an experiment   _____design a mural

_____produce a videotape   _____write a song

_____develop an interactive computer presentation

_____create a series of sketches, diagrams, or graphic organizers

_____other _____

This would be a good way to demonstrate understanding of this concept because:

_____

_____

To do this project, I will need help with:

_____

_____

Action Plan: _____

_____

_____

_____

_____

The criteria/rubric that will be used to assess the finished product is:

_____

_____

_____

My projected completion date is _____

Student Signature _____ Date ___/___/___

Teacher Signature _____ Date ___/___/___

Second Grade
Fire Safety Project

Plan with your family the procedure you should follow should there be a fire in your home. Your plan must include the points listed below, which we talked about and practiced in class. You may record your plan to present to the class using **a video, diagram, model, song, written report, or photo essay.**

Include the following points:

1. Check closed doors before opening.

2. Stop, drop, and roll.

3. Stay down, close to the floor.

4. Have two ways of evacuation.

5. Know what to do if both ways are blocked.

6. Establish a family meeting place.

Nancy Reece, West Irondequoit Central School District, Rochester, NY

General Science Space Project

Choose one of the projects listed below to further explore space and to demonstrate what you have learned during our space unit.

1. The school newspaper is doing an article on space exploration and the editor has asked you to create a **timeline** to go along with the article. Your timeline is to include major events in space exploration and discovery from the time of Sputnik until the present. Each event should have a brief explanation and a **visual** of some sort.

2. You are a realtor selling vacation condos on an orbiting space station. Create some sort of **advertisement** that will be seen across Indiana to convince people why they would want to buy a space station vacation condo. Your ad can be for a magazine, newspaper, or TV.

3. You are an astronaut on the space shuttle. Write a **letter** home to your family detailing how you get by doing day-to-day activities without gravity and with Newton's laws in full effect. Include in your letter **pictures** of where you go about these activities.

4. Mr. Wizard is doing a TV show on space exploration. You are to write a **song** to be performed on the show about all of the important explorations into space since Sputnik

5. Create a new **board game** (you may use any available game board) about the history of the space program. The board game will be played in class as a review activity of the space chapter.

6. You are a TV news anchor doing a series on how the space program has impacted the lives of everyday people. **Research** man's first landing on the moon and the Challenger disaster. **Interview** some people on how those two events impacted their lives. In some way, recreate the interview for your classmates to see.

Jeanne Galbreath, Jennings County High School, North Vernon, IN

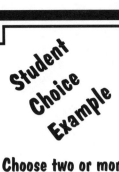

A Look at the Theater

Choose two or more of the following projects for your further study of the theatre.

PROJECT POSSIBILITIES:

1. Write an original play or TV drama of your own.

2. Study a playwright. Suggested authors:

    Lorraine Hansberry: *Raisin in the Sun*   Neil Simon (free choice)

    Carson McCuller: *Member of the Wedding*   Andrew Lloyd Webber (free choice)

    Arthur Miller (free choice)   Thornton Wilder: *Our Town*

    Read two plays written by the playwright, a biographical sketch, and either a play review or a feature story about the author. Write a 4-5 page paper on his or her contribution to the theater.

3. Attend a play. Write a critical review or prepare and present a radio or television review.

4. Read and analyze a play by Shakespeare and see the movie version. Design a project that compares the two versions.

5. Research the history of the musical comedy in the U.S. Write a paper or prepare a multi-media presentation for the class.

6. Read a play concerning a famous person and compare it to a biography of that person. Use a paper, oral report, or artistic presentation to make your comparison. Suggestions:

    Clarence Darrow: *Inherit the Wind*   Helen Keller: *The Miracle Worker*

    Anne Frank: *The Diary of Anne Frank*   Franklin D. Roosevelt: *Sunrise at Campobello*

7. Read a book that is a source of a musical. Study the musical and give a written, oral, or artistic presentation comparing the two. Suggestions:

    Anna and the King of Siam and <u>The King and I</u> or *Don Quixote* and <u>Man of LaMancha</u> or *The Once and Future King* and <u>Camelot</u> or *Oliver Twist* and <u>Oliver</u> or *The Matchmaker* and <u>Hello, Dolly!</u>

9. Read the live theater sections of the newspaper for a month. Clip reviews, feature stories, and advertisements of plays. Make a handbook of local theater offerings, including a brief commentary about each clipping. Also include a list of theaters and dinner theaters in this area.

10. With others, give a puppet or marionette show. Write a script and make the puppets.

11. Adapt a favorite short story, book, or comic strip into a play or musical. Write a script OR songs OR choreograph dances OR design sets and costumes for the production.

12. Write a paper on the history of drama, including the Greeks, medieval pageant plays, and modern theater. Use correct research form and at least four sources.

OR... Design a project of your own. Please check with me before beginning the project.

Adapted from unknown source.

Revolutions Unit Test

Directions: Choose one project from part A and one project from part B.

Part A: Choose one of the following Revolutions and complete one of the three assignments.

Scientific Revolution or Enlightenment   **Glorious Revolution**
French Revolution   **Industrial Revolution**

1. **Political Cartoon w/caption** -- Draw a political cartoon explaining the viewpoint of one of the sides involved in the revolution you have chosen. (State on back of your cartoon which side you are taking; it does not necessarily have to be your viewpoint.)

2. **Newscast** -- In news format, chronicle the events that occurred during this revolution. You may use visuals to enhance your newscast. You are required either to perform it for the class or to videotape it for me in order to get credit. (Computer-generated visuals are acceptable.)

3. **Flip Chart** -- Chronicle the major historical events of this revolution by using a flip chart of graphics and facts. (Computer-generated are acceptable.)

Part B: Choose one of the following V.I.P.s from a revolution other than the one you chose above (i.e., if you chose the French Revolution, you may not choose Napoleon, Robespierre, or Louis XVI), and complete one of the three assignments below.

Any Philosopher   **Louis XVI**   **Napoleon**   **Marie Antoinette**
Oliver Cromwell   **James I**   **Charles II**   **William & Mary**
Adam Smith   **Robert Owen**   **Karl Marx**   **Sir Isaac Newton**
Robespierre

1. **Biopoem** -- Write a biography of your chosen leader by writing a poem about their policies and/or accomplishments. Enhance your poem by including personal information as well.

2. **Job Application** -- HELP WANTED: Seeking person with revolutionary ideas. Develop an application that would ask all pertinent questions to find the perfect person for the job. Then choose one of the people above to fill out the application. Answer it in the voice of the person, based on what you have researched about him/her.

3. **Wanted Poster or National Hero Poster** -- Draw (do not download photo) your chosen leader and, in advertisement format, tell why this person is/was considered a villain or a national hero. Use factual information. This is similar to the mini-wanted posters we have done, only more information is required.

Lynn Butler and Lorraine Fusare, Rush-Henrietta School District, Henrietta, NY

Interest Grouping

Giving students a voice in how they will access and process new learning, and how they will demonstrate that learning, appeals to their ever changing interests and to their need for independence. If these decisions have been entirely teacher-centered, you can start with a limited array of choices and gradually increase the options as students are independently able to choose productive learning experiences for themselves.

You can interview students, use interest inventories, and just listen in and observe to gather data about what choices might be of interest to them. Your knowledge about multiple intelligences theory, as well as the extensive list of potential perspectives and products found in the chapter on assignments, should make this match up between student interest and assignments an easy one to accomplish. The form *How I'll Show You What I Know* can serve as a template for students to use in identifying their preferences.

If you want to be explicit about gathering some data about influences and interests, these questions can provide a starting point:

1. What books, movies, or television programs make you think? Why do you think that is so?

2. If you could live in another place, where would you live and why?

3. What is the best/most exciting/most memorable moment you have had so far in your life?

4. If you could meet three famous people, who would you want to meet and why? What would you want to ask them?

5. If you could live in another time period, what time period would it be and why?

6. If you could chose any person in the world to have dinner with, who would you choose and why?

7. Given five choices, have students rank order any of the following: classes, recreation activities, times of the year, toys, vacation sites or activities, sporting events, best places to eat or live, school activities, television shows, or movies.

No matter what questions you choose, **patterns of interest** will begin to emerge. This information will enable you to design individual choices and plan group assignments around similar interests, as well as plan meaningful stories and examples to use in instruction.

Top 10 List Jigsaw Research

If, when you do a **TASK ANALYSIS** you discover that many of the students lack the background information they need to make sense of material they are about to study, the necessary information can often be generated by the students in short order.

Have the students **generate a list** of what they would like to know about a topic, time period, region of the world, concept, etc. The **Three Column Chart** or **All Hands on Deck Brainstorming** can be a useful tool in this process.

Have the media center staff prepare a **book cart** for use in the classroom, raid storage closets, and have students bring in any materials they have at home related to the topic to be studied.

Assign or have each student select a subtopic; this is a great opportunity for **interest grouping!** Ask each student to prepare a list of ten things they learned about their topic in their research.

Cluster students by topic and have them share their individual lists. Have the groups then generate their group's **Top Ten Lists** of facts about the information they have gathered. Provide large pieces of chart paper and markers to each group so they can write out their lists complete with pictures, charts, graphs, and/or artifacts as appropriate.

These can be shared with the entire class by posting and having students do a **Walking Tour** or by **group reports** on the background information.

By taking the time to do this gathering of background information "upfront," students will have **"velcro"** on which to hang the more complex information you want them to learn during the unit.

Anchoring Activities

Anchoring Activities are the activities students work on as they enter the classroom, when they are finished with other assigned work or any other potential "down time." These activities "anchor" students to continuous learning if the activities are matched to standards and district guidelines.

Points to Note:

❀ These activities can be done individually or in small groups.

❀ Use old materials (cut up worksheets and workbooks, assignments you no longer use, etc.) in a new way to avoid massive teacher preparation.

❀ Think about how the anchoring activities can be translated into a second language or have the emphasis shift from math to science to language arts with a slight change in the directions.

❀ Change the target audience (younger children, classmates, parents, pen pals, etc.) to completely change the nature of the assignment.

❀ **Design anchoring activities that match your state and district standards or program of studies,** the learning styles and interests of your students. Create exercises for remediation or extension purposes, OR let the students select from or create a new menu.

Possibilities...

Best Sellers List

Make a list of the five best books for students of this age to read. Write a brief description of each book and tell why each is such a good book. Students and teacher can put together a composite list of the books and send it home for a summer reading list.

School Improvement

Make a list of ten things that could be changed in your school that would make it a better place to learn and work; provide supporting rationale. Students and/or teacher could put together a master list and identify projects on which to work.

Anchoring Activities continued...

Spelling Spectacular

Make a list of all the spelling words students of this age (or studying this subject) should know or of the words it would be fun to know how to spell. Words can be used for a variety of classroom activities such as cooperative spelling lessons, categorizing by known spelling rules, by parts of speech, by similarities or differences, etc.

Standardized Test Preparation

Identify standardized test areas (SAT, ACT, SRA, IGAP, ISTEP, Iowa, Terra Nova, Regents, etc.) and prepare independent packets for shoring up weak areas or areas not emphasized in the standard course of study.

Research Race

Long Term Anchoring Activity

Contest Rules:

- In the fishbowl, you will find dozens of folded slips of paper. Each slip contains a question about the world around us. Multiple resources are available around the room to help you locate the requested information.
- Choose a slip from the fish bowl and answer the question found on the slip.
- Use 5"x7" index card for writing answer.
- Use the question as the title.
- You can earn 50 points for each information card you complete.
    - Each grammatically correct sentence (no more than six sentences) 5 pts
    - Quality of information: accuracy and completeness 10 pts
    - Neatness of product 5 pts
    - Bibliography information presented in correct format 5 pts

All Month! Learning! Fun! Prizes!

Plate Tectonics
Tiered Assignment Example

Complete a total of four assignments from the list below. For the first three, choose one assignment from each level. Be sure that each choice is a different letter. The fourth assignment is your choice, but it must be a different letter than the other three. Scoring is based on total points scored out of a maximum 100 possible points.

L E V E L   O N E

A. Describe the stages of mountain development and the characteristics of each stage. Give one example of the location of mountains at each stage.

B. Construct a diagram of the complete rock cycle; compare and contrast each of the three (3) types of rocks according to a written list of three (3) of your own criteria.

C. Investigate and provide an imaginative explanation for the simile: The rim of the Pacific Ocean is like a "ring of fire."

D. Write a letter to a friend expressing your thoughts and concerns about a recent 7.0 magnitude earthquake that occurred in her city at a longitude opposite of yours. Provide for her a "scientific" explanation for the cause of the earthquake. Also explain why you did not feel it.

Each choice from this level is worth a possible 10 points.

John Banker, Rush-Henrietta High School, Heneritta, NY

Plate Tectonics continued...

Remember: Complete a total of four (4) assignments. Choose one (1) assignment from each level. Be sure that each choice is a different letter. The fourth (4th) assignment is your choice, but it must be a different letter than the other three.

LEVEL TWO

A. Construct a poster of a cross-sectional diagram of at least five (5) sedimentary rock layers. These layers formed within the same geologic era but are of different absolute ages; they are also intruded with a dike and a sill. The age and type of each rock layer must be shown.

B. Develop a hypothesis that explains the relative and absolute ages of the Hawaiian islands. Support your hypothesis with at least three (3) lines of scientific evidence.

C. Develop a design for an "earthquake-proof" high rise building or bridge. Or speculate on the likelihood of a major earthquake occurring in Southern California. Describe the earthquake's cause and ways damage might be controlled or reduced.

D. Suppose you are an old, lifelong, wilderness resident of the north slope of Mt. St. Helens. The date is May 16, 1989. Write a diary entry describing your decision to stay, or leave, the mountain. Include at least three (3) reasons for your decision.

Each activity at this level is worth a possible 20 points

LEVEL THREE

A. Construct a chart showing and explaining three (3) types of plate boundaries and describing the features found at such areas that result from plate movement.

B. Research the Himalayan Mountains. Develop a classification system based on their characteristics and process(es) of formation. Identify other mountain ranges that fit your classification system.

C. Speculate on the scientific validity (relative to that period in history) of Alfred Wegener's original theory of continental drift. Add to it at least two (2) explanations of more current discoveries that will serve either to support or refute the theory.

D. Imagine that you are a geologist working in a seismology lab at the University of Rochester. Develop some imaginary earthquake data and an analysis of that data to calculate your distance for the earthquake's epicenter. Describe what you do and how you feel when you locate the epicenter near the residences of two of your closest friends or relatives.

Each choice from this level is worth a possible 35 points.

John Banker, Rush-Henrietta High School, Heneritta, NY

A Doll's House

Within assigned groups, students work together to answer questions about Ibsen's *A Doll's House*. While suggested materials and end outcomes may vary, each group's responses should reflect research, reading, and group discussion.

Group 1

Questions:
1. Why is *A Doll's House* considered the first modern drama? What specific changes did Ibsen make to the traditional form of drama?
2. How does the play structurally differ from Sophocles' *Antigone?*

Materials:
- Selected reviews/critical essays
- Biographical information on Ibsen
- History of the theater (All information in library/Internet)

Outcome:
1. Using a detailed timeline visual, show the evolution of drama from *Antigone* to *A Doll's House*.
2. Explain Realism and show its effect on the play using specific examples.
3. In the voice of Ibsen, write a 1-2 page response explaining why you made such drastic changes.

Group 2

Questions:
1. What was middle-class life like in Norway in the 1870's? Which aspects of it are evident in the play?
2. What were the expected gender roles?
3. How does literature reflect a society's view of relationships, the roles of women and men?

Materials:
- Information on 19th century life in Norway
- Selected literary works (All information in library/Internet)

Outcomes:
1. Prepare a presentation in which you answer questions 1 and 2 using visuals, overheads, etc.
2. Using two works of literature, write a 1-2 page paper in which you illustrate the authors' attitude toward gender expectations.
3. Write a letter in the voice of either Nora or Torvald in which you give that character's definition of a "perfect spouse."

Jeff Guercio, Irondequoit High School, West Irondequoit Schools, Rochester, NY

A Doll's House
continued...

<table>
<tr><td>

Group 3

Questions:

1. What positive and negative reactions did the critics have to the play? What were their concerns?
2. Does Ibsen's "alternative ending" address their concerns? Is it an effective solution? Does it change the meaning, intent, or spirit of the work?

Materials:

- Clement Scott's review
- Additional critical responses
- Ibsen's alternative ending

Outcome:

1. Share the critics' view of the play by assuming their roles and addressing the class as such.
2. In a 1-2 page response, evaluate the effectiveness of the alternative ending.
3. Write a letter to Mr. Scott either defending or refuting his critique of the play.

</td><td>

Group 4

Questions:

1. What was Ibsen's response to the critics of his play *A Doll's House*?
2. What social statements does he make through his play *An Enemy of the People*? Do you see any connections to *A Doll's House*?

Materials:

- Ibsen's *An Enemy of the People*
- Biographical information on Ibsen

Outcome:

1. Provide the class with a synopsis of the play *An Enemy of the People* and explain how it was Ibsen's response to his critics.
2. Write a 2-3 page paper in which you compare author Henrik Ibsen to his character Dr. Stockman in *An Enemy of the People*.

</td></tr>
</table>

Jeff Guercio, Irondequoit High School, West Irondequoit Schools, Rochester, NY

Managing
Differentiation of Instruction

Each week the teacher selects work for each student to complete.
THE STUDENTS DECIDE WHAT WORK TO DO WHEN.
Kathy Vogt reports that this opportunity for choice is "highly motivating" for students who quite often find reasons to avoid doing their work.

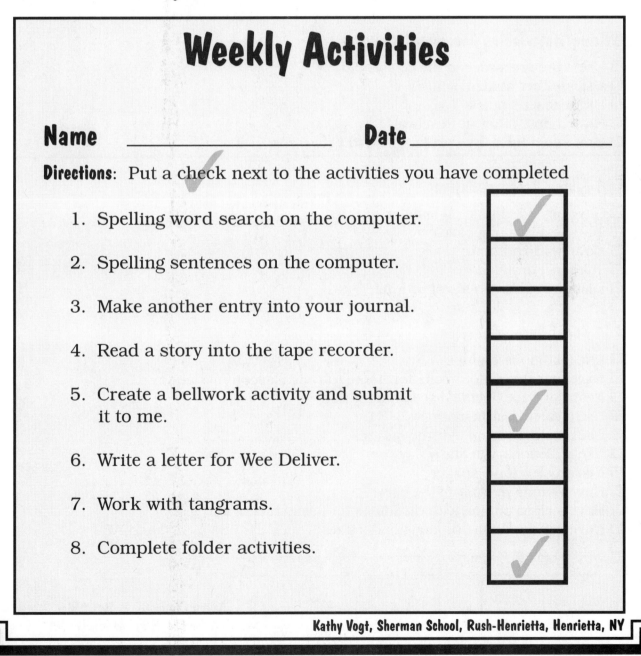

Weekly Activities

Name _____ **Date** _____

Directions: Put a check next to the activities you have completed

1. Spelling word search on the computer.

2. Spelling sentences on the computer.

3. Make another entry into your journal.

4. Read a story into the tape recorder.

5. Create a bellwork activity and submit it to me.

6. Write a letter for Wee Deliver.

7. Work with tangrams.

8. Complete folder activities.

Kathy Vogt, Sherman School, Rush-Henrietta, Henrietta, NY

Accommodation Request Form #1

Student:

Teacher:

Monitor Teacher:

Date:

Writing/Note-Taking Accommodations

☐ Use a tape recorder in the classroom
☐ Use another student's notes
☐ Use teacher's notes
☐ Have a note-taker in the class
☐ Use a computer, typewriter, or word processor

Test-Taking Accommodations

☐ Have extended time on tests or quizzes
☐ Take test in a quiet area
☐ Have test read orally
☐ Take test orally
☐ Dictate answers to a test or quiz

Additional Accommodations

☐ Use textbooks-on-tape
☐ Have an extra set of books for home (physical accommodation)
☐ Restroom use (medical accommodation)
☐ Use a calculator in class
☐ Use a calculator on tests or quizzes
☐ Use a dictionary in class
☐ Use an electronic speller
☐ Have seating in front of the class
☐ Have a class outline with due dates for assignments and tests
☐ Have extended time on nonstandard tests such as: PSAT, SAT, and ACT
☐ _____
☐ _____

Adapted from J.E.B. Stuart High School
Fairfax County Public Schools, VA

Accommodation Request Form #2

Student:

Subject:

Teacher:

Monitor Teacher:

Date:

1. When you need extra help in class, which of these are most likely to help you?

☐ Taped lectures   ☐ Extra time on assignments
☐ Class notes   ☐ Taped textbooks
☐ Using a word processor   ☐ Alternative tests/assignments
☐ Asking questions during a lecture   ☐ Joining a study group

2. When preparing for a test or exam, which of these accommodations would be most helpful to you?

☐ Asking for extra time on the test   ☐ Asking to take the test in another room
☐ Asking to have the test read to you   ☐ Asking for writing assistance
☐ Asking to read your answers into a tape recorder

3. If you have reading difficulties, which of these are most likely to help you?

☐ Asking to have textbooks taped   ☐ Asking for someone to read to you
☐ Asking for study guides   ☐ Enrolling in a reading skills class

4. If you have writing difficulties, which of these are most likely to help you?

☐ Using a computer for word processing   ☐ Asking for proofreading help
☐ Dictating written work to someone   ☐ Asking to give oral reports
☐ Asking for a note-taker   ☐ Tape recording lectures

5. If you have math difficulties, which of these are most likely to help you?

☐ Asking for extra explanations   ☐ Listing steps of a process in your notes
☐ Using graph paper   ☐ Using a calculator
☐ Setting up time to work alone with the teacher

6. If you have trouble with organization, which of these are most likely to help you?

☐ Asking for a syllabus/course schedule   ☐ Getting assignments ahead of time
☐ Keeping a calendar of assignments   ☐ Breaking large assignments into parts

Adapted from R. E. Lee High School
Fairfax County Public Schools, VA

Thinking Skills
for the
21st Century

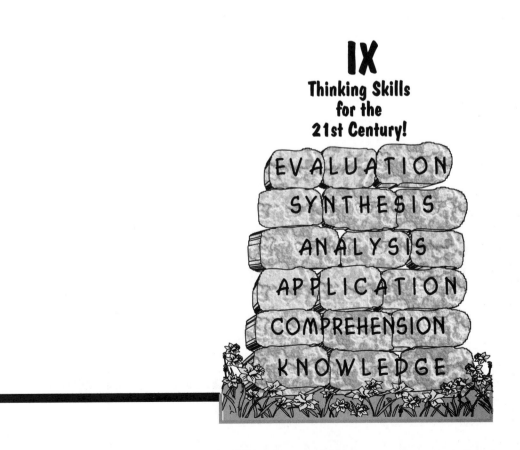

IX
**Thinking Skills
for the
21st Century!**

EVALUATION

SYNTHESIS

ANALYSIS

APPLICATION

COMPREHENSION

KNOWLEDGE

TOP TEN QUESTIONS
to ask myself as I design lessons

1. What should **students know and be able to do** with what they know as a result of this lesson? How are these objectives related to national, state, and/or district standards or proficiencies?

2. How will **students demonstrate what they know and what they can do** with what they know? What will be the **assessment criteria** and what form will it take?

3. How will **I find out** what **students already know,** and how will I help them access what they know and have experienced both inside and outside the classroom? How will **I help them** not only **build on prior experiences**, but **deal with misconceptions** and **reframe their thinking** as appropriate.

4. How will new knowledge, concepts, and skills be introduced? Given the diversity of my students, what are **my best options for sources and presentation modes** of new material?

5. How will **I facilitate student processing (meaning making)** of new information or processes? What are the key questions, activities, and assignments (in class or homework)?

6. How will **I check for student understanding** during the lesson?

7. What do I need to do to **differentiate instruction** so that the learning experiences are productive for all students?

8. How will I **"Frame the Learning"** so that **students know the objectives**, the **rationale** for the objectives and activities, the directions and procedures, as well as the **assessment criteria** at the beginning of the learning process?

9. How will I build in opportunities for students to make real world connections and to learn and use the varied and complex thinking skills they need to succeed in the classroom and the world beyond?

10. What adjustments need to be made in the **learning environment** so that we can work and learn efficiently during this study?

Thinking Skills for the 21st Century...

Collaborative Thinking Skills

Organizational Thinking Skills

Remembering
Summarizing
Metacognition
Goal Setting & Planning
Formulating Questions
Developing Hypotheses
Learning How to Learn
Problem Solving
Decision Making

Critical Thinking Skills

Using Inductive & Deductive Thinking
Determining Reality & Fantasy
Predicting Benefits &Consequences
Identifying Values, Ideologies & Bias
Distinguishing among Fact, Opinion, &
    Reasoned Judgement
Determining the Accuracy of Information
Judging Essential & Incidental Evidence
Determining Relevance
Identifying Missing Information
Judging the Credibility of a Source
Recognizing Assumptions & Fallacies
Identifying Unstated Assumptions
Detecting Inconsistencies in an Argument
Identifying Ambiguity
Identifying Exaggeration
Determining the Strength of an Argument

Creative Thinking Skills

Fluency
Flexibility
Originality
Elaboration
Imagery
Curiosity
Brainstorming
Creative Problem Solving

Introspective Thinking (Knowing Self)

Analytical Reasoning Skills

Identifying Characteristics
Recognizing Attributes
Determining Critical Attributes
Making Observations
Comparing & Contrasting
Categorizing & Classifying
Criteria Setting
Ranking, Prioritizing, & Sequencing
Pattern Finding
Predicting
Determining Cause & Effect
Making Analogies

Systems Thinking Skills

Thinking Skills for the 21st Century
Organizing the Learning Environment to Teach Of Thinking, About Thinking, & For Thinking...

Of Thinking

Learning experiences are designed so that thinking processes are named, modeled, and practiced in a variety of situations. A goal of this approach is for students to establish a thinking skills repertoire that they can access purposefully and independently.

About Thinking

The learning environment is structured so that students reflect on their own thinking; they are taught to be aware of the kinds of thinking required in particular subjects and situations. They are asked to monitor the effectiveness of their thinking.

For Thinking

The learning environment is structured so that all skill building and information input leads to opportunities to make personal meaning and connections to life beyond this particular moment and beyond the classroom. There are opportunities to respond to and ask thought provoking questions.

!

Aha!

???

Teaching for Thinking...

Top 10 Historical Changes
from the
Age of Transition

Your Task

You have been hired to edit a new history textbook. Your boss, the publisher, wants a rank ordering of the top ten historical changes during the Age of Transition.

Your publisher has given you a list of ten events that have occurred during the Age of Transition. Now, your job is to rank order these events according to your group's criteria for which event is more important than another. Use the process described on the next page.

Age of Transition Events

- Machiavelli's *The Prince*

- Gutenberg's invention of the printing press

- Galileo's findings with the use of the telescope

- Martin Luther's posting of the 95 Thesis

- Columbus' discovery of the New World

- The Commercial Revolution and the invention of capitalism

- Henry VIII's creation of the Anglican Church

- Calvin's predestination

- Rebirth of Greek and Roman ideas and culture

- The theory of mercantilism

Age of Transition continued...

Process

In your group:

1. **Discuss each event in your group's list.**

   Use the attached sheet to:

   a. List the event

   b. Write an explanation of the impact this event had on history (both short term and long-term). Remember the most important information for your group's ruling will come from your assessment of the impact of each event.

2. **Discuss the criteria you will use to decide which event ranks first, second, etc.**

   a. Using the criteria sheet, list the priorities you will use. Example: When I asked myself what reasons I would use to rank one event higher than another, I thought that maybe events that had an effect on the largest number of people might be valued higher than ones that affected a limited region or area.

   b. Possible criteria include, but are not limited to, the following:

   • What reasons will I use to decide which event ranks first, second, etc.?

   • How will I decide which events had the most impact on history?

   • Will I rank the events that had the most positive effect on man's life first... or the events that had the most economic impact...?

   • What criteria will I use to decide which event ranks first, second, etc.?

3. **As an individual, rank the ten events, using the sheet provided.**

   a. Use your criteria to guide your placement of each event.

   b. Be sure you have a rationale (reason) for placing the events in the order you have rated them.

   c. Be prepared to share your reasons with the class during a class discussion/activity.

Tamara Lipke, Irondequoit High School, Rochester, NY

Finding A Balance Between
Skill Building and Meaning Making

**Just because learners use a
skill doesn't mean they know which
skill they are using!**

**They need multiple opportunities to reflect about and
label the skills they are using.**

**Just because students use a skill doesn't mean they recognize
where else that skill can be used!**

**They not only need to use skills in a variety of situations, they need
to focus on where else they might be able to use that skill both
inside and outside the school setting.**

**Just because learners can name and define the skills they're using
doesn't mean they know how to use those skills well or efficiently.**

**Learners also need to reflect on the usefulness of each of the skills,
and analyze what actions or behaviors were
the most effective and why.**

Skill Building & Meaning Making for Me...

1. What should I know and be able to do at the end of this lesson/unit or experience?

2. What do I already know that will be useful in learning this new material or working in this way?

3. How is this knowledge and are these skills important in the world outside of school?

4. When are the important check points and deadlines?

5. How will I be able to tell when I have done a really outstanding job?

4th Grade Daily Learning Log
for the week of _____

M O N D A Y

Things I Learned

1.

2.

Opinion of My Day

Something On Which I Want to Work Harder & What I Plan To Do

T U E S D A Y

Things I Learned

1.

2.

Opinion of My Day

Something On Which I Want to Work Harder & What I Plan To Do

W E D N E S D A Y

Things I Learned

1.

2.

Opinion of My Day

Something On Which I Want to Work Harder & What I Plan To Do

T H U R S D A Y

Things I Learned

1.

2.

Opinion of My Day

Something On Which I Want to Work Harder & What I Plan To Do

Stacy Holahan & Margie Cawley, Sherman School, Rush-Henrietta School District, Henrietta, NY

4th Grade Reflections on the Week

Name: Week of:

What I Learned This Week:

How I Can Use It:

Areas in Which I am Making Progress:

I Need to Improve In:

My Goal for Next Week:

What I Enjoyed Most This Week:

Parent's Signature and Comments:

Stacy Holahan & Margie Cawley, Sherman School, Rush-Henrietta School District, Henrietta, NY

Teaching for & about Thinking
Interactive Notebooks

One of the most exciting innovations to promote student processing of new learning is the **Interactive Notebook** described in Addison Wesley's **History Alive!** and widely used by teachers of history and other social sciences. The uses of the **Interactive Notebook** extend to all areas of study because the structure and potential contents capture the essence of active participation, multiple intelligences, and the variables of the brain-comptable classroom.

To get started with the **Interactive Notebook** process, ask students to purchase and bring to class each day an 81/2 by 11 inch spiral notebook with at least one hundred pages and a container holding a pen, a pencil with an eraser, at least two felt tip pens of different colors, and at least two highlighters of different colors. Other desirable equipment includes a small pair of scissors and a glue stick. If the cost is prohibitive for some students, create classroom supply kits.

Students are taught productive methods of notetaking during lectures, readings or other presentations that they record on the **RIGHT side of their notebooks.** They are encouraged to vary size of letters, boldness of letters, use of capital letters and lower case letters, indentations, underlining, bullets, colored markers, and highlights in the notetaking process.

The **LEFT side of the notebook** is reserved for student processing of the information recorded on the **RIGHT** side. Students can be asked to review and preview, draw maps, think of a time when..., summarize in a sentence, create graphic organizers, create a metaphor, respond to "what if" questions, take a stand. Additionally, encourage them to add newspaper clippings or political cartoons, drawings and illustrations, or other such personal touches. The use of color and visual effects is highly encouraged! The **LEFT,** or processing side, can be completed in class or as homework.

Text Organizational Patterns

Almost all nonfiction books are presented in one of, or a combination of, these five text structures. TEACH FOR THINKING by teaching your students to recognize the structure and to use the graphic organizer that is best for organizing the important information presented in the text.

Classifications and taxonomic listings focus on information about different concepts/facts that are classified according to a specific set of criteria. Signal words are "there are several types," and "one subset of this issue is...." The visual that looks like an organization chart or family tree is a useful graphic organizer for this pattern of text.

Sequential and chronological text patterns present a series of events in chronological order, or the sequential steps of a process. Information in history texts is often presented chronologically, while information in science is often presented as a sequence of stages. Signal words for this text structure are "first," "next," "then," and "following that." Flow charts are best for capturing the important bits of information in this text structure.

Compare and contrast text patterns identify items with similarities and/or differences. Signal words for this text structure are "similarly," "likewise," "contrary to," and "unlike." Venn diagrams and matrices are useful graphic organizers with this pattern.

Cause and effect text patterns are used when two events or items are related to each other, with some causing an event and some resulting from the event. Signal words for this pattern include "as a result of...," "consequently," and "therefore." The graphic organizer with the "event" in the middle, with causes flowing into the event and the effects flowing out, is useful with this pattern.

Expository or descriptive text patterns present a series or list of facts, ideas, or variables that may not immediately seem to be related to one another, or may seem to jump from one point to another. Mind maps or semantic maps and webs are useful in clustering the information.

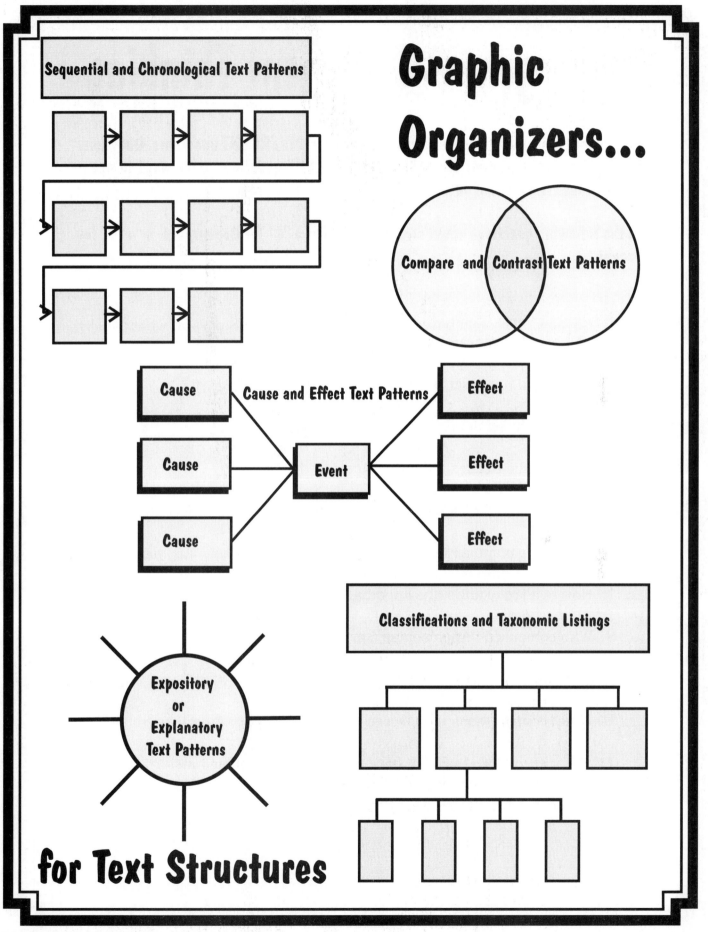

Graphic Organizers...

Sequential and Chronological Text Patterns

Compare and Contrast Text Patterns

Cause

Cause

Cause

Cause and Effect Text Patterns

Event

Effect

Effect

Effect

Classifications and Taxonomic Listings

Expository
or
Explanatory
Text Patterns

for Text Structures

Convergent & Divergent Thinking

Questions that have more than one correct answer are **DIVERGENT** questions. Questions with only one correct answer are called **CONVERGENT** questions. We want to use a balance of these two types of questions in our instructional programs.

Mark the following questions about music with either a "C" for Convergent or a "D" for Divergent.

_____ 1. Leonard Bernstein based the musical "West Side Story" on what play by William Shakespeare?

_____ 2. How would you describe the music of Andrew Lloyd Weber?

_____ 3. What are the sections of a symphony orchestra?

_____ 4. How did the Beatles influence music in the '60s?

_____ 5. How are marching bands and drum and bugle corps different?

_____ 6. Why is the piano a member of the percussion family?

_____ 7. How is a jazz combo like a football team?

_____ 8. Who composed "Appalachian Spring?"

_____ 9. Who followed Arthur Fiedler as conductor of the Boston Pops?

_____ 10. What contributions did George Gershwin make to American music?

_____ 11. What effect does the MTV have on American popular music?

_____ 12. When was the electric keyboard invented?

Bloom's Taxonomy: Definitions and Examples

Evaluation
Examine all parts of a concept in order to evaluate or assess it. Judge the significance of a problem.

Read an article & evaluate the author's argument. Listen to debate & judge which side presented the best argument.

Synthesis
Combine a new concept with what you already know in order to construct new knowledge. Compose, design, rearrange, plan.

Combine the ideas presented in several readings about the death penalty with your ideas to develop your argument.

Analysis
Able to separate the new concept into its parts and understand their relationships. Compare, contrast, analyze, identify. Recognize patterns.

Identify the author's 3 main arguments in an assigned article. Analyze a song by separating it into its parts.

Application
Able to use the new concept to solve problems. Able to apply the concept in a situation that is different from that in which the concept was first learned.

Develop a chart showing 5 things computers can do but people cannot. Use the Spanish verbs you just learned in 5 sentences.

Comprehension
Able to explain or restate ideas in own words. Translates and interprets. Able to use the new concept as a building block for further learning.

Summarize the author's point of view. Restate the poem in your own words.

Knowledge
Recognize and recall facts. Able to repeat what was learned or follow rules. Material learned in this manner may be remembered long enough for a test, but until understood, it can't be used as a foundation for further learning.

Recite the periodic table. Memorize ten Latin nouns. Define metaphors.

Bloom's Taxonomy
Question & Task Design Wheel

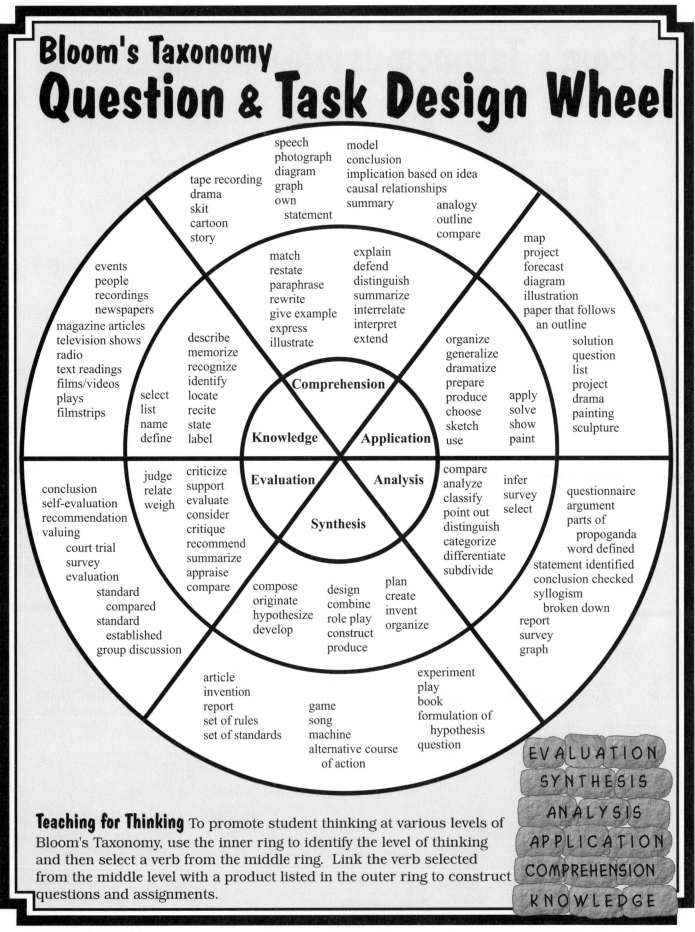

Teaching for Thinking To promote student thinking at various levels of Bloom's Taxonomy, use the inner ring to identify the level of thinking and then select a verb from the middle ring. Link the verb selected from the middle level with a product listed in the outer ring to construct questions and assignments.

Bloom's at Work!

EVALUATION
SYNTHESIS
ANALYSIS
APPLICATION
COMPREHENSION
KNOWLEDGE

Identify the level of each of these tasks.

_____ List the departments of the Executive Branch that are headed by cabinet level positions.

_____ Based on our research, discussions, and your own personal knowledge, how might the cabinet be reorganized to function more efficiently.

_____ Compare and contrast the areas of responsibility of the Secretary of State and the Secretary of Defense.

_____ Select three cabinet level departments and summarize the primary responsibilities of those positions in your own words.

_____ Justify or criticize the suggestion to eliminate the Department of Education.

_____ Using the information you obtained in your readings, create a graphic organizer that shows the organization of the Department of the Treasury.

Bloom's Taxonomy
Don't underestimate the power of the knowledge level!

1. The higher levels of the taxonomy are not necessarily "better" than the lower levels. Evaluation without knowledge and comprehension can lead to faulty decisions. Do not underestimate the importance of the knowledge level. Learners need to master the following as part of the educational process:

Knowledge of Specifics

Knowledge of Specific Facts

Knowledge of Terminology

Knowledge of Theories

Knowledge of Principles & Generalizations

Knowledge of Trends & Sequences

Knowledge of Universals

2. Higher level questions are not necessarily more difficult than lower level questions. For divergent thinkers focusing on the details required for knowing and comprehending can be a difficult task; they would prefer to create new versions or render judgments about the information.

3. The use of certain process words will not necessarily guarantee a particular questioning level. If you have told them "why" and then ask them "why," the question is at the recall or knowledge level.

4. Don't get "too hung up" on the particular level of the question so that you lose sight of the overall value of the need for different levels of questioning. There is clearly overlap in the levels because one builds on the other. Analysis and application require solid knowledge and comprehension.

EVALUATION

SYNTHESIS

ANALYSIS

APPLICATION

COMPREHENSION

KNOWLEDGE

Williams' Taxonomy of Divergent Thinking & Feeling

Fluency is a thinking skill that allows a thinker to generate many ideas.

Flexibility is a thinking skill that allows the learner to adapt everyday objects to fit a variety of categories by taking detours and varying size, shape, quantities, time limits, etc.

Originality is a thinking skill that allows the learner to seek a unique or not so obvious use or twist by suggesting unexpected changes.

Elaboration is a thinking skill that allows the learner to expand, add on, enlarge, enrich, or embellish a list of ideas in order to build on previous thoughts.

Risk Taking is a state of mind and skill that allows the learner to explore the unknown by taking chances, experimenting with new ideas, or trying new challenges.

Complexity is a competency or skill that allows the learner to be "multi-tasked," to deal with intricacies, competing priorities or events, and to create structure in an unstructured setting or bring logical order to chaos.

Curiosity is a way of thinking that allows the learner to follow a hunch, to inquire, question alternatives, ponder outcomes, and wonder about options.

Imagination is the capacity to fantasize possibilities, build images in one's mind, picture new objects, or reach beyond the limits of the practical.

Teachers' Guide to Williams' Taxonomy

Fluency:
Name as many_____
as you can in 60 seconds.

Flexibility:
Classify the_____listed in
the fluency exercise. Use a
unique classification system.

Originality:
Think of
a unique way to...

Elaboration:
Explain what you think
it would be like today
if...

Risk-Taking:
If you compared yourself
to a _____, what kind of
____ would you resemble?

Curiosity:
If you could meet a/an
_____, what would you
want to know about...?

Complexity:
Describe or design an
object or machine that you
could make from_____.

Imagination:
Imagine that _____
could talk. What would they
say to/about...?

Mary Ackley, Rush-Henrietta Central School District, NY

Williams' Taxonomy at Work!

Stretch your mind by answering these questions about the United States of America and then identify the kind of thinking or feeling required for each answer.

Name as many states as you can in two minutes. _____

How might the United States be different if it was discovered west to east? _____

Classify the states listed in the first item by some system other than location or size. _____

Imagine that the states' capitols could talk. What would they say about people? _____

Think up an original name for a new state. _____

If you compared yourself to a state, what state would you resemble? Give three reasons why you are like that state. _____

Explain what you think our society would be like today if each state was a country. _____

If you could meet the governor of New York, what would you want to know about how the state is run? _____

Stacey Russotti, West Irondequoit Central Schools, Rochester, NY

Teaching for Thinking...
Concept Attainment Model

Purposes:

To develop inductive thinking skills

To practice identifying patterns and forming hypotheses

Set-Up:

Identify the concept to be studied.

Locate positive and negative examples of the concept. A minimum of twenty sets of examples is recommended with at least two-thirds positively representing the concept.

Sequence the examples starting with several positive examples.

Procedure:

Phase One:

Inform learners that they will see positive and negative examples of an idea you want them to discover.

Present data to the learners in pairs and label the data sets as positive or negative examples.

Ask students to develop hypotheses about what attributes or patterns they are seeing. Prompt them to try out several hypotheses and extend their thinking by focusing attention on specific features of the examples.

Track and record on the board or chart paper the possibilities they generate and delete those proven incorrect by the presentation of additional examples.

Have students name the concept and the rules or definition of the concepts according to their attributes. If the students do not know the name of the concept, provide the name in phase two when student hypotheses are confirmed.

Phase Two:

Students confirm their thinking about the concept by:
  a. correctly identifying additional unlabeled examples of the concept as positive or negative
  b. by generating their own positive examples

Phase Three:

Students analyze the processes and strategies they used, what they did when strategies did not work, and whether or not they explored more than one hypothesis at once, etc.

Hilda Taba's
Inductive Thinking Model

Stage One: Concept Formation

Phase One: Creating and listing of data set

Phase Two: Grouping of data

Phase Three: Labeling and categorizing of data

Stage Two: Integration of Data
(Interpreting, Inferring, and Generalizing)

Phase Four: Identifying relationships

Phase Five: Exploring relationships

Phase Six: Making inferences

Stage Three: Application of Principles or Ideas

Phase Seven: Predicting consequences and hypothesizing

Phase Eight: Explaining and/or supporting the predictions and hypotheses

Phase Nine: Verifying predictions

Implementation Guidelines

- Teachers may organize the data set or have the students create and organize the data set. If time is limited, the process can be shortened by teacher preparation of the data.
- During the process, teachers ensure that the stages occur in the right order. It is common for students to try to label the categories and then try to force items into their prenamed/predetermined categories.
- Teachers plan and ask questions designed to help students move to the next stage at the appropriate time.
- When first using the process, the teacher decides when to move on to the next phase; as students gain experience with the model, they can make decisions about when to move on to the next phase.
- Props, or other visual cues, help to focus students on the topic to be studied. For example, when the lesson is based on current events, the covers of newsmagazines can be posted to remind students of specific events and of the kinds of events that make the news as they generate the data set.

Teaching for Collaborative Thinking...
Jigsaw Cooperative Learning

Set-Up

1. Identify content that could be divided into segments and taught by students to other students.

2. Divide the material to be studied into meaningful chunks. Identify the number of segments of material to be learned and place the same number of students in each base group. (Three to five segments/students in a group is workable.)

3. Assign a segment of the material to be learned to each person in the base groups. Each person in the base group has different material to study.

Student Tasks

4. Each student studies his/her material independently. (This can be done in class or as homework, depending on the material and age of the students.)

5. Students meet in "expert" groups to study the material and to plan how to teach it to their base groups. (All the 1s who have independently studied the same material meet together, the 2s meet together, etc.) This segment is crucial because you want to be sure that the "expert" groups are identifying important/significant points; it is often helpful to prepare "expert sheets" for the groups to use in their planning.

   You can build in requirements for visuals and planned checks for understanding.

6. Students return to their base tables and teach the material they studied independently and in their expert groups to their base group.

Jigsaw Cooperative Learning continued...

Assessment &

Individual Accountability

7. Ensure individual accountability by some means. This can range from a traditional quiz to Numbered Heads Together to a random oral check for understanding.

Helpful Hints:

If this process is completely new to your students, use it first with simple content. A general rule of thumb is to avoid, when possible, introducing complex material and complex processes at the same time.

Analyze the interpersonal/communication skills needed for your students to work successfully in this way. Identify which skills they have and which you will need to explicitly teach prior to their working in two different cooperative groups.

Provide opportunities for the students to discuss, not only their learning about academic content, but how they worked together in their groups.

Decisions! Decisions!

In column 1, list three **situations** in which you made a choice today.

In column 2, tell what your **choice** was.

In column 3, give the **reasons** why you made that choice.

In column 4, tell whether you think you made the **right choice or not.**

1 Situation	**2** Choice Made	**3** Reason	**4** Evaluation

Decisions! Decisions!

1. Define the Problem: _____
_____
_____

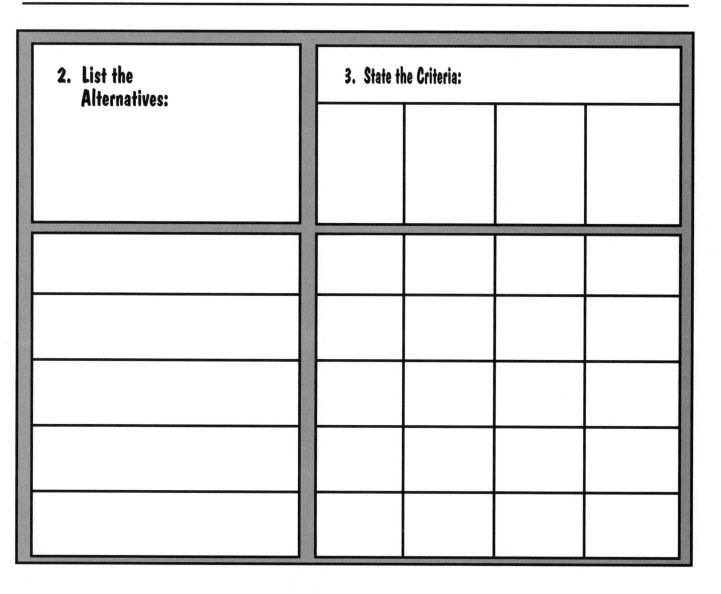

2. List the Alternatives:

3. State the Criteria:

4. **Evaluate the alternatives:** Place a plus (+) opposite each alternative and under each criteria that you believe is desirable. Place a minus (-) opposite each alternative and under each criteria that you believe is undesirable. Place a question mark (?) opposite each alternative and under each criteria that you believe is neither desirable nor undesirable.

5. **Make your decision:** Write your decision and the reasons for your decision below.

_____
_____
_____
_____

Teaching for Thinking...
Inquiry/Problem Solving Model

Steps in the Inquiry Model

› **Identification of a content-based question/problem**

› **Presentation of the question/problem**

› **Formation of hypotheses**

› **Gathering data**

› **Analysis of data and formation of conclusions**

Putting the Inquiry Model to Work

Identification of a content-based problem

The **problem/question** that serves as the basis of an inquiry lesson may surface as a result of ongoing study, or it may be identified by teacher and/or students as an appropriate focus of study. Teachers and students working in a **standards based classroom** often organize their study on **essential questions** that are complex and, more often than not, have more than one "right" answer. This process is a powerful one for focusing student learning on the essential questions.

Presentation of the problem

The use of an **anticipatory set** or **props** helps students focus the problem. This increases the likelihood that students will make connections between this problem and their life experiences.

Present an explicit statement of the problem/question orally and in writing.

Formation of hypotheses

Students may spontaneously volunteer **hypotheses**, as well as respond to questions or prompts from the teacher or the student leading the process.

Inquiry/Problem Solving Model continued...

Gathering data

In many instances, the teacher organizes the **data-gathering** process. As students build skills in organizing the process, more responsibility can be turned over to them.

Who does the gathering of the data depends on the age of the students, the complexity of the problem, and the amount of time the teacher wants to spend on the **inquiry process** as compared to the time spent on the **content.** Teacher gathering of data can make the problem-solving process seem easier to the students than it really is, but that may be a small price to pay if it allows the teacher to add inquiry learning opportunities to his/her instructional repertoire.

The data gathering may take place in the classroom setting, or it may be completed individually or in small groups outside the classroom. Data gathering outside the school setting helps promote the idea that inquiry and problem-solving are not just school work, but are rather the work of real life.

Analysis of data and formation of conclusions

This is a difficult task and students may need **modeling** and/or **coaching** in order to get the most out of this phase.

The data can be organized in a variety of ways. Students can be taught to use **graphic organizers** to organize data so it can be evaluated and patterns identified.

Original hypotheses need to be revisited, revised, and perhaps eliminated, if the data does not support original conclusions.

Analyze the Learning Environment for selected SCANS Skills and Competencies

WHAT IS IN PLACE (or needs to be in place) THAT PROMOTES:

Creative Thinking:

Decision Making:

Problem Solving:

Seeing Things in the Mind's Eye:

Identification, Organization, and Allocation of Resources:

SCANS Analysis continued...

Evaluation of Information:

Systems Thinking around Organizational, Social, and Technological Systems:

Negotiation, Teaching, Persuasion, and Team Building:

Fort Worth Public Schools' Vision of a SCANS Classroom

More than one solution may be viable, and the teacher may not have it in advance.

Students routinely work with teachers, peers, and community members.

Students and teacher plan and negotiate activities.

Students routinely assess themselves.

Information is acquired, evaluated, organized, interpreted, and communicated by students to appropriate audiences.

Organizing systems are complex; teacher and students both reach out beyond school for additional information.

Disciplines needed for problem-solving are integrated; listening and speaking are fundamental parts of learning.

Thinking involves problem-solving, reasoning, and decision-making.

Students are expected to be responsible, sociable, self-managing, and resourceful; integrity and honesty are monitored within the social context of the classroom; students' self-esteem is high because they are in charge of their own learning.

Source: Fort Worth Public Schools

The Learning Environment

The Learning
Environment:
Learning How
to Learn

All too often we are
giving young people
pieces of fruit when we
should be teaching
them to grow their
own plants.

TOP TEN QUESTIONS
to ask myself as I design lessons

1. What should **students know and be able to do** with what they know as a result of this lesson? How are these objectives related to national, state, and/or district standards or proficiencies?

2. How will **students demonstrate what they know and what they can do** with what they know? What will be the **assessment criteria** and what form will it take?

3. How will **I find out** what **students already know,** and how will I help them access what they know and have experienced both inside and outside the classroom? How will **I help them** not only **build on prior experiences**, but **deal with misconceptions** and **reframe their thinking** when appropriate?

4. How will new knowledge, concepts, and skills be introduced? Given the diversity of my students, what are **my best options for sources and presentation modes** of new material?

5. How will **I facilitate student processing (meaning making)** of new information or processes? What are the key questions, activities, and assignments (in class or homework)?

6. How will **I check for student understanding** during the lesson?

7. What do I need to do to **differentiate instruction** so that the learning experiences are productive for all students?

8. How will I **"Frame the Learning"** so that **students know the objectives**, the **rationale** for the objectives and activities, the directions and procedures, as well as the **assessment criteria** at the beginning of the learning process?

9. How will I build in opportunities for students to make **real world connections** and to learn and use the **varied and complex thinking skills** they need to succeed in the classroom and the world beyond?

10. What adjustments need to be made in the learning environment so that we can work and learn efficiently during this study?

The Classroom IS the REAL WORLD!

When twenty to forty people of an any age spend 180 plus days together in a relatively small space, careful attention must be paid to how property, space, time, and human interactions are handled. First, think of the issues facing any group of people spending that much time together and consider the instructional pieces after you've clarified how this society should function.

Use all you have ever learned about etiquette, group process, conflict resolution, problem solving, personality types, safety, time management, etc. when considering how to set up the learning environment. The classroom should be as much like life beyond the classroom as possible. The students are real people, who just happen to be a little younger than the teacher, and who have been ordered to report to your care. If you are inclined to set up a dictatorship, be prepared to deal with stealth attacks and/or revolutions; if, however, you are interested in establishing a more democratic type setting, be clear what the parameters are. Not only must you be clear, you must clearly communicate those boundaries to the students as all of you collaborate to create an effective and efficient learning environment.

Tips for Surviving and Thriving Together

➤Use inclusive pronouns; i.e., "our" classroom not "my" classroom.

➤Become a world class listener!

➤Learn how to send assertive messages...and teach students to do the same.

➤Be aware of all that is going on but make thoughtful decisions about when and how to react to inappropriate situations.

➤Use and teach students to use processes for decision making, problem identification and solving, and conflict resolution.

➤Keep both feet on the ground. You are the adult! As Fred Jones says, "It takes one idiot to backtalk; it takes two to make a discussion out of it."

➤Practice what you preach!

➤Catch them being right!

➤Remember that kids are people too. Sometimes they are simply acting their age rather than like the "little adults" we think we want them to be.

➤View discipline problems as human relations problems and react accordingly.

Ways to Let Students Know You Believe
They are Capable of Achieving at a High Level

1. **Communicate clear expectations.** Include criteria for success such as rubrics, task performance lists, & exemplars of good performance.

2. **Model enthusiasm for what is to be learned, the work to be done, & for student effective efforts & successes.**

3. **Organize the learning environment FOR thinking.** Carefully plan questions, craft examples, stories, & activities that promote transfer & retention.

4. **Monitor student attributions & use attribution retraining** with those who make external attributions.

5. **Provide feedback from multiple sources** so that learners are able to learn from the feedback & make adjustments in their future work.

6. **Design a brain compatible classroom** through the use of active learning, feedback, and varied sources of input in a safe environment.

7. **Coach students in setting challenging yet attainable goals & in designing & implementing action plans for attaining those goals.**

8. **Include opportunities for all categories of thinking** in discussions with & assignments for low performing students. Teach students to think **ABOUT their thinking** & to learn what kind of thinking is required in which situations.

9. **Promote & teach effective effort strategies:**
    - task & error analysis
    - choice of sources, processes, & products
    - focus groups for skill development
    - graphing of progress
    - interactive notebooks
    - journal/log entries (cause & effect of effort)

10. Once unit & lesson objectives are clear, plan how you will **differentiate instruction** so that all students can successfully process learning & demonstrate mastery of the objectives.

Development of the intrapersonal intelligence causes one to examine the effectiveness of one's effort. Teaching students to assess what works and what doesn't work for them in the learning process may be the most important thing we teach them. Younger children believe ability and hard work combine to promote success. As students get closer to adolescence, they tend to believe that those who succeed are smart or are just plain lucky; one thing they "know for sure" is they do not want to be caught trying, because if they fail, everyone will know they are dumb! This perception for them is a reality that greatly impacts their willingness to expend effort. **Attribution retraining** can make a huge difference in the lives of our students.

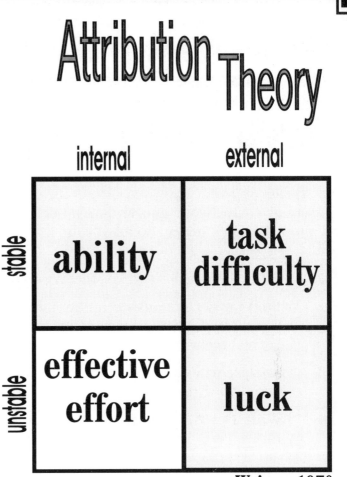

Attribution Theory

	internal	external
stable	ability	task difficulty
unstable	effective effort	luck

- Weiner, 1970

Attribution Retraining

A learning environment where students learn how to learn includes opportunities for students to reflect on their efforts and to learn from their errors. Successful adults know that it is the effectiveness and efficiency of effort that determines how well we reach the goals we set for ourselves. Our tendency is to tell students this "fact of life" rather than systematically teaching them by our modeling and by insisting that they analyze their own work.

The single most effective way to respond to students who say the task was too hard, or they were unlucky, or they are just too dumb is to say, "Given that you believe/think/feel that..., what might you do about it?" The least effective response is to try to confuse them with logic by pointing out how unclearly they are thinking; they will not buy it. Allow them to see the world as they see it AND create conditions that cause them to consider how they might do something to improve the results in the future. For example, catch them being right and point out that effort must have played a part, mention that you work hard to prepare interesting and challenging lessons, and include recognition of effective effort in your verbal and written praise.

Making the Most of Errors...

Error Analysis

You may correct your quiz and earn back at least 1/2 of the points you missed. Follow the steps below. Do all of your work on your own notebook paper. This is due: _____.

1. Write the problem and/or the word you missed.

2. Find the correct answer and write it down under the problem and/or word you missed. Write a brief statement about how or where you found the correct answer or solution.

3. Analyze why you missed the problem or work originally. Write a statement about your reasons.

4. Write 1 or 2 sentences explaining how you can prevent this mistake in the future.

Example

1. **JARGON: I gave an incorrect definition of this word.**

2. **JARGON is defined as being a vocabulary specific for a particular field of study. I found this definition in my notes from class.**

3. **I believe that I missed this word because I didn't study correctly or enough. I also think I get a little nervous when I take a test and can't remember some of the things I studied.**

4. **I think that I need to go through my notes and make a list of all the words that I don't really know and the words my teacher has indicated might be on the quiz. I need to then give myself a "practice test" on those words. I might need to make flash cards of the words I have trouble remembering. If I still have problems with tests or quizzes, I will see my teacher for help.**

Lynne Gronback, McDougle Middle School, Chapel Hill-Carrboro Schools, Chapel Hill, NC

Error Analysis Chart
multiple assignments

Name _____

Period _____

Date	Assignment/ Assessment	Score	Added Wrong	Multiplied Wrong	Used Wrong Operation	Dropped a Negative Sign	Did Not Distribute Number	Copied Incorrectly	Mistake in Formula	Did Not Follow Directions	Incomplete	Cancelled Wrong	Skipped the Problem	Other (Specify)

Directions:
For each assignment or assessment completed, write the name of the assignment and the date on the lines to the left. Check as many types of errors in each row as apply.

Contract for Improvement Points

Name:

Class Period: Date:

Title of Work to be Improved:

I,   agree to re-work/re-write the work named above. I will improve the work by addressing the following specifics agreed upon by my teacher and myself. The points I might earn have been assigned & I understand that I must complete the work according to the contract requirements in order to receive full credit.

Specific Improvements   **Points Possible**

1.

2.

3.

4.

5.

6.

Date Improved Work Due: **Total:**

Signatures:

©Just ASK Publications, ASK Inc.

Lynn Gronback, McDougle Middle School, Chapel Hill-Carrboro Schools, Chapel Hill, NC

Incomplete Assignment Log

Title of
Assignment:

Name:

Date:

Period:

I did not complete this assignment because:

My plan for meeting the requirements is:

Space, Time & Procedures 101
for a Productive Learning Environment

Space

Arrange the space to reduce barriers between you and the students and to help them see and hear one another. Match the room arrangement to the instructional objectives and to the interactions you wish the students to have.

Small group/cooperative work: **Tables or clusters of desks or chairs**

Class discussion: **Circle or horseshoe with teacher seated as part of the group**

Test taking: **Rows**

General overall best arrangement: **Horseshoe or double horseshoe**

When using the whole class question-answer strategy or a class discussion, expect students to speak loudly enough for everyone to hear the response throughout the classroom. If the response is not loud enough, ask the student to repeat the answer so everyone can hear it. As a general rule, avoid repeating it yourself or your voice will dominate the discussion.

Time

Give students time to process and time to think before calling on someone or before responding to a student response. Too often, we are uncomfortable waiting for a response and want to hurry on to the next question. As a result, many students realize that they can just "watch the action" and do not even attempt to participate; others with word retrieval problems often find themselves at least one question/comment behind. As Pat Wolfe says, **"Learning is not a spectator sport."** This means that we need systems for purposefully building in time for students to think.

Procedures

Procedures/routines that are not followed are simply **dreams** and routines that are blindly followed become **ruts**. Constantly check to see how expensive your classroom procedures are in terms of time and energy. Maximize your efforts by honestly assessing what needs to be changed, added, or deleted.

Time Templates

in a learning environment where students learn how to learn

Wait Time: Pause three to five seconds after asking a question to give all students time to process the question. Pause three to five seconds again, after a student answers, so you and the other students can process the response and the responding student can add more as appropriate.

"Learning is the constant; time is the variable."
...Vermont teacher

10:2 Theory: Pause after small meaningful chunks of information for student processing. Have pairs or trios discuss the most important points, confusing points, connections, etc.

Sequence: We remember best that which occurs in the first few and last few minutes of instruction. Maximize that time. Create lots of beginnings and endings. That which is just after the middle of a list is the hardest to remember. When possible, reorder the list to place the difficult items at the beginning or end.

Movement: Legitimize movement. The brain can only absorb what the rear end can endure. Have students stand for the two minute processing in 10:2. Have students move to meet with a partner or use various signals to indicate understanding or agreement.

Practice: Divide new skills into the smallest meaningful chunks and mass short practice sessions at the beginning of new learning. Always move to real and meaningful use of the skills as soon as possible.

Time Templates continued...

Forgetting: Most forgetting occurs within just a few minutes of learning. Build in recitation, review, processing, and practice immediately.

Notice: Warn students of upcoming transitions. Think of the "two minute warning" before the end of football games and do the same in the classroom.

Pacing of Speech The more complex the concept and the more unfamiliar the vocabulary, the slower the pace needs to be.

Pacing of Lesson: Attention spans are short, so provide variety of learning experiences.

So students can learn how to use time effectively, share with them how you make instructional decisions related to time and ask them to consider the implications for their independent study.

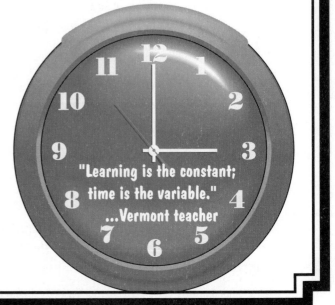

"Learning is the constant; time is the variable." ...Vermont teacher

Wait Time

Mary Budd Rowe's research indicates that slowing down the questioning pace actually speeds up the pace of learning. We tend to rush through question and answer sessions because "We have so much to cover!" and because we fear that moments of silence will lead to off task behaviors. She recommends that **we pause for three to five seconds before calling on students to answer the questions we pose and before responding to their answers to our questions**. This sounds easy, but it takes determination and practice!

One tip for remembering to incorporate this quality thinking time is to ask the question from the front of or from one side of the classroom and walk slowly to the opposite side before selecting a student to respond. A way to deal with "blurters" is to acknowledge students who indicate that they wish to respond by signaling each of them a number in order of recognition. When most students have indicated their readiness, select a number at random and call on the student who was assigned that number.

To engage all students in thinking about and responding to important questions, you might use **Think-Pair-Share**, as described on page 104, since the think time is built-in wait time. Many teachers have found that the use of **slates, think pads or white boards** (page 111), or **signal cards** (page 109) helps reprogram them and their students to pause for processing.

What Wait Time Accomplishes...

- Students ask **more questions.**

- Student to student **interaction increases.**

- The length and number of **student responses increases.**

- **Contributions by "low performers" increase.**

- The need for **management actually decreases** because more students are engaged.

- **Failures to respond decrease.**

- **Teacher ask more higher level questions and ask more follow-up questions.**

Procedure Potpourri

Planning procedures and evaluating the effectiveness of those procedures for conducting the business of the classroom is crucial in creating a productive learning environment. **Read** through the regularly occurring events listed below. **Describe** the procedures currently in place in your classroom and **rate** their effectiveness. In rating, consider the time and energy each is costing you and the students, as well as the results achieved. If the record keeping or the "nag factor" is too time and energy consuming, then either the procedure or the process for implementing the procedure needs to be adjusted. **Identify** which procedures need rethinking and/or reteaching in order to maximize their effectiveness.

Entering the classroom

Beginning the school day or the class period

Taking attendance

Returning from absences

Dealing with tardies

Procedure Potpourri continued...

Distributing materials

Collecting materials

Dealing with broken or missing supplies, restroom visits, drinks, etc.

Asking for and receiving help

Making transitions

What to do when work is finished

Leaving the classroom

Procedure Potpourri...add your own ideas!

Procedure for...

Procedure for...

Procedure for...

Potential Problem Times...

Careful thought and attention to detail in advance is essential for these moments. It is best to have "Plan B" ready to roll on a moment's notice, because even those procedures that have been working well up until this time may fall apart here! Do not be surprised and do not take it personally!

➤The day(s) before a big holiday or school break

➤The day of or the day after Halloween

➤The day report cards and/or progress reports are distributed

➤The first few minutes after a long weekend or holiday

➤Friday afternoons before a three day weekend

➤The last week of school (especially if the swimming pools are open and/or it's hot)

➤Immediately before or after a pep rally or assembly

➤Right after a fire drill

➤The last few minutes before lunch & the first few minutes after lunch

➤The first substitute of the year

➤Power outages

➤First snow of the year (especially in Florida)

Dealing with Discipline

in a productive and positive learning environment

Focus on finding fault. Instead, catch students being right!

Use awards for good behavior. Students begin to work for the reward rather than because the work is interesting or the behavior is the right thing to do.

Ask students to make promises. They often promise anything to get us off their backs.

Nag, scold, and threaten. These may lead to immediate compliance, but there is high potential for resentment and frustration.

Be overly concerned about your own authority base. Real authority comes from knowing what you are talking about and modeling respectful behavior.

Use double standards. The same standards should apply for students and teachers.

Identify causes of inattentive or disruptive behavior and match your response to the perceived cause.

Communicate clearly your expectations for work and behavior.

Focus on future behavior rather than on past behavior.

Establish a relationship based on trust and mutual respect with each child.

Discipline problems are human relations problems. React accordingly!

Dealing with Discipline continued...

Wait to hold discussions about inattentive or disruptive behavior, or unmet expectations until both of you are calm.

Use logical consequences directly related to the behavior. Logical consequences are designed to get students back to work.

Teach that fairness has to do with equity rather than equality.

Distinguish between the behavior and the person exhibiting the behavior. Build self-efficacy by focusing on what effort is needed.

Admit your own mistakes.

Remember that responsibility is taught by giving responsibility. Include students in developing procedures for handling inappropriate behavior or unmet expectations.

WHEN THE GOING GETS ROUGH...

Stay calm, move slowly, get close, be quiet and relax.

Make eye contact.

If you must talk, lower your voice rather than raising it.

Try to keep the situation in perspective. Don't overreact and escalate minor incidents into major confrontations.

Avoid public confrontation. An audience for a confrontation escalates any differences.

Avoid threats you can't or don't want to carry out.

Adapted from Mamchur

Top 10 Questions for Secondary Teachers

1. What **choices** do students have around **sources of information, processes for making meaning, and for demonstrating their learning?**

2. How often do **students feel in control**, in charge of themselves? What causes them to feel in control? Think beyond "They decide whether or not to get involved and to do the work."

3. What **decisions** that really count are students allowed to make? Consider issues like pacing, contracts, order of study, and depth and breadth of particular areas of study.

4. What structures are in place to help students learn how to be **responsible for their own learning?** Think of issues like error analysis, lessons to be learned from errors, rubrics, self, peer and group assessment, time management and study skills lessons, and reflections.

5. How do your students know **(beyond grades)** when they have pleased you?

6. How do you know when **you have pleased them?**

7. How purposeful are you in planning and asking questions that have more than one right answer? **How often do the students ask you and each other complex questions?**

8. How often do students feel important in your classroom? **What makes them feel important?**

9. How often do you and your students share laughter and pleasure?

10. How do the students react when they walk into your classroom? Happy? Calm? Safe? Excited? Assured? Afraid? Bored? Sorry? **What goes on in this learning environment that contributes to that reaction?**

"In all my 25 years of teaching secondary students and training teachers, I have never known teachers who are having trouble with discipline or motivation to say that their students have choices, control, or true responsibility for their own schooling."

Carolyn Mamchur, "But... the Curriculum," *Phi Delta Kappan*, **April 1990**

Collegial
Collaboration

XI
Collegial Collaboration

In most organizations things tend to get done
because of **RELATIONSHIPS**, not through
job descriptions or formal roles.

Collegial Collaboration
Practices that Promote School Success

Educators who use their knowledge, skills, and energy to...

- analyze standards and design instruction and assessments to match those standards
- design and prepare instructional materials together
- design and evaluate units together...especially those based on clearly articulated national, state, or local standards
- research materials, instructional strategies, content specific methodologies, and curriculum ideas to both experiment with and to share with colleagues
- design lesson plans together (both within and across grade levels and disciplines)
- discuss/reflect on lesson plans prior to and following the lesson
- examine student work together to check the match to high standards and to refine assignments
- agree to experiment with an idea or approach, to debrief around how it worked, and to analyze the results and make adaptations and adjustments for future instruction
- observe and be observed by other teachers
- analyze practices and their productivity
- promote the concepts of repertoire and reflection
- teach each other in informal settings and in focus groups
- use meeting time for discussions about teaching and learning rather than administrivia
- talk openly and often about what they are learning or would like to learn
- concentrate efforts and dialogue on quality and quantity of student learning, rather than on how many chapters have been covered in the text

greatly increase the probability of higher student achievement.

framed by the research of Judith Warren Little

Ways to Strengthen Collegiality

1. **Rotate faculty meetings or department meetings to different classrooms.** The teacher who is hosting the meeting shares with the group something he/she is working on in her teaching. This can last five minutes or an entire faculty meeting.

2. Arrange for a **substitute for twenty specific Wednesdays** during the year who can cover classes for teachers who are observing one another. Line up the same person for all the peer observation and conferencing days. If possible, have the substitute prepare lessons around an enrichment topic valued by the entire school so that the teachers who are observing one another won't have to prepare lesson plans. Possible topics include safety, study habits, the environment, diversity, thinking skills, music and/or art appreciation. (Saphier)

3. Include activities such as **"Stir the Faculty" or "Mail Call"** in staff meeting agendas.

4. Model and include **small group processing and interaction in faculty meetings.**

5. **Have principal or other "special" staff teach classes** so a grade level team can meet or teachers can observe one another.

6. Begin each faculty and/or department meeting with **brief discussions of instructional strategies.**

7. **Duplicate articles** and place them in each others/teachers' mailboxes.

8. Have teams of **teachers lead department or staff meetings.**

9. Expect that **all conference/workshop attendees report back** to the faculty and/or departments about ideas gleaned from the conference/workshop attended.

10. Organize and participate in **focus/study groups.**

11. Create systems for **asking for help and providing one another assistance** through group process and problem solving.

12. Open doors and file cabinets to one another...hold a **swap shop.**

13. Create a **"What's New Board"** for faculty lounge or office. (Saphier)

14. **Openly recognize and applaud those promoting collegiality.**

Learning Clubs

Learning Clubs are small groups of teachers who meet regularly to discuss their lives as teachers. During a learning club meeting, **each teacher takes a turn** discussing some aspect of her teaching life. In running her part of the meeting, the teacher selects one of four kinds of discussion:

1. Review

The teacher asks the group to focus on an instructional strategy they have studied together and explain how it is working in each of their classes. The discussion would focus on issues of how it worked and what they learned from their initial attempts to use the strategy.

2. Problem Solving

The teacher presents a problem he is currently facing and asks the group for help in clarifying the problem and brainstorming possible actions to take. A structured problem solving model will yield the best results.

3. Now Hear This!

The teacher announces that she wants to use her time to either share a success story about a recent or current instructional encounter, or to complain about a dilemma she is facing. In a "Now Hear This" session, the group members' responsibility is to appear interested and use active listening. They do not offer solutions or suggestions.

4. Lesson Design

The teacher asks the group to help plan a lesson or unit, or to review a plan he has designed.

After a teacher has announced what kind of help he wants, and the group has focused on his issues for approximately 15 minutes, his turn ends and another teacher begins her turn by declaring what kind of session she wants. Once each group member has had a turn, the group spends five to ten minutes discussing the ideas shared during the meeting and the implications of each for their professional practice.

adapted from *TEAMWORKS! Building Support Groups that Guarantee Success*, by Slev and Gottlieb, Warnerbooks, NY, 1989

3-D Teams
Data Driven Decision Teams

Groups of teachers meet once or twice a month to review and analyze student work in an effort to use data to make solid instructional decisions. The analysis, reflection, and collegial collaboration provides a framework for decision making about future instruction. This practice is a particularly useful tool for teachers who are striving for consistency across classrooms in a standards based learning and assessment environment.

The group members bring samples of student work to the meeting. Hanson, Silver and Strong, in descriptions of their Authentic Achievement Teams, suggest that each teacher bring six pieces of students' work to the meeting; they further recommend that the samples represent different achievement levels or different levels of success on this particular assignment. For example, two might be from the top third of a class, two from the middle, and two from the bottom. An alternative approach would be to analyze the work of "regular" students and that of ESL, advanced, or inclusion students. It is also helpful to bring copies of any directions given to the students.

If the group members have not planned together, ten to fifteen minutes is spent looking through the student work samples and any teacher artifacts so that all participants get a good idea of what kind of work they will be discussing and analyzing.

The participants can agree to analyze all the work of their students around the same set of criteria, or each teacher can indicate the questions, concerns, or criteria to be considered for that set of student work. In either case, the outcomes of the discussion might be directed toward:

➢ checking for **validation** about the appropriateness of the work for the developmental stage of the students

➢ checking to ensure that the task is **congruent** with the stated mastery objective and/or state or district standards

➢ checking for **consistency** of opinion about the assessment and evaluation of the work

➢ possible **adjustments** in teacher directions and **support** for all/some of the students.

Focus Groups

Focus Group Meetings

These meetings are opportunities for educators to spend dedicated time in the discussion of classroom practice. These discussions usually include the presentation or demonstration of new strategies or areas of study and the sharing of action research in the classroom.

Logistics

Meeting time varies from thirty minutes to two hours. If the group has more than eight to ten members, break into smaller groups for discussions of issues and action research. Multiple sessions on the same topic facilitates follow-up discussion after classroom implementation.

Meeting Formats

Presentation and Demonstration

The group leader, a member, or a guest presents an instructional technique and demonstrates it. Follow-up discussion is focused on implications for classroom practice.

Magazine/Book Club

Prior to the meeting, group members all read an article or a chapter in a jointly selected book. The meeting revolves around a discussion of the book and the implications for classroom practice. An alternative is to have each member of the group bring a different article related to a group identified issue or to have each member read a different book. Each participant then shares a review of that article/book over a series of meetings. Once again, discussion focus is on implications for classroom practice.

Brainstorming and Problem Solving

Group members brainstorm responses to a common problem such as students coming late to class, poor performance on homework, how to explain a concept the learners have trouble grasping, etc. Each group member picks an alternative from the list to try before the next meeting.

Curriculum Discussions

Teachers share techniques or discuss ways to teach a particular subject/concept. The standards movement makes this particular type of focus group an important one. Each member agrees to try this method of instruction and to report back on the outcomes for student learning.

Collegial Discussions

Use these questions to structure your discussions about what you did differently in your classroom as a result of your previous focus group, learning club, or workshop. Anyone in the group may pose the questions.

1. What You Tried:

Give a brief description of the strategy(ies) you tried. Identify the standard on which the learning was focused and explain why you chose to use this strategy.

2. How It Went:

Successes Experienced:
- What worked well?
- What pleased you?
- How were you able to know that the use of this process helped achieve the desired learning?

Problems Encountered:
- What frustrated you?
- Was the process a good one for the content to be learned?
- Were there any logistical problems?

3. What You Learned:

Possible Revisions
- What changes might you make when you use this strategy again?
- What revisions would deal specifically with the problems you encountered?

Critical or Interesting Incidents:
- How did your behavior, or that of your students, match what you expected?
- What intrigued you?
- What questions were raised in your mind?

4. Next Steps:

- Where do you go from here? Where might you use this strategy next?
- What do you need to do to remember to use this strategy again?
- With whom should you share your success/the usefulness of this strategy?
- With whom could you problem solve?

adapted from Geoff Fong & Ray Szczepaniak, Department of Defense Dependent Schools (DoDDS), Europe Region

Points to Ponder in Reflective Discussions or Journals

These questions may be helpful in guiding your reflections on your practice. Whether you feel the day/class went well or you feel that you'd like to do the whole thing over, you owe it to yourself to analyze what worked or didn't...and why. It may be your preference to debrief with a colleague, or you may prefer to make journal entries in a beautiful notebook or on your word processor. The format does not matter; it is the gift of reflection that you give yourself that is so valuable.

Did you frame the learning in such a way that students:
➤ knew which standards or proficiencies were the focus of the learning?
➤ knew what they were to do and how what they were doing related to important and essential learning goals?
➤ were able to make connections to past learning and experiences, and to life beyond the classroom now and in the future?
➤ were able to be successful in completing the assigned tasks and make meaning of their work?

Did you establish a safe, nonthreatening environment where:
➤ students felt safe taking risks, admitting confusion, and dealing with errors as learning opportunities?
➤ your interactions with students and the interaction between students were positive and sometimes even humorous?
➤ student sense of self-efficacy and inclusion was enhanced?
➤ inappropriate student behavior was redirected in a private and productive way?

Did you create productive learning environment by:
➤ circulating around the classroom and calling on as many students as possible?
➤ communicating with each student with either non-verbal or verbal language?
➤ carefully planning thought provoking questions and maintaining an appropriate balance between levels of thinking required by the questions?
➤ practice wait time after questions and after answers?
➤ using modeling or modeling thinking aloud for key points in the lesson?
➤ providing clear examples, analogies, metaphors, or stories to convey important ideas?
➤ considering learning styles and multiple intelligences in designing the lesson?

Did you build in processing/meaning making time by:
➤ checking for understanding on multiple occasions?
➤ practicing 10:2 theory?
➤ having students summarize their learning either orally or in journal entries?

adapted from Michael D. Koehler

Dynamic Discussions About Teaching...
Let's Hear It for Peer Coaching & Peer Poaching!

NO ONE questions the power of peer observation!
EVERYONE seems to question the reality of finding the time (and training) to do it well!

The full process of conferencing prior to and following a peer observation is highly encouraged. If, however, you have yet to find the time and training to engage in peer observation, there is no reason to delay any longer. **Discussions about teaching prior to delivery of instruction, classroom observations, and discussions about teaching after delivery of instruction are valuable in their own right.** Coaching, practicing good communication skills, problem solving, reflective questioning, and observing are a part of our professional lives each and every day. The next step is asking for and providing one another the same support we provide our students.

Ideas for what you and a colleague might discuss prior to, or following, an observation are offered for use within the complete process or in isolation. Choose from this menu and add your own. Don't delay. It is the cheapest and most accessible form of staff development available to you. Go for it!

Thought Provoking Questions to Discuss Before an Observation

What is it that you want students to know and be able to do as a result of the lesson today?

How is this related to district or school standards or priorities?

Where are you and your students in this particular unit of study?

What kinds of related and important learning experiences have occurred during the past few weeks in your class?

How do you intend to follow up on those experiences during the next week?

What activities will you have the students engaged in during this lesson? Why did you select these activities for use at this time?

Dynamic Discussions continued...

What do you expect your students to learn from each of these activities?

Do you plan to use the text? In addition to the text, what materials or resources will you use to present the concepts and have students process their learning?

How will you determine whether or not your students have learned what you want them to learn during the lesson? At the conclusion of the unit of study?

As you currently see the lesson, what will be the sequence of events?

When will transitions from whole class instruction to small group work occur?

How will student movement be built into the learning activities?

As you see the lesson unfolding, what exactly will students be doing?

What do you see yourself doing to make all this happen? Do you envision any particular problems or confusions?

Given that the class period is an extended instructional period, how do you plan to chunk activities during the ninety minutes?

Are there any special circumstances in the classroom that affect learning/the learning environment? What do you do to accommodate those circumstances?

Does any particular student, or group of students, within this class present special challenges? How are you dealing with them?

Starting Points for Discussions Following the Observation

As you look back on the lesson, how do you think/feel it went?

What happened that makes you think/feel that way?

What do you remember about your actions during the lesson?

What do you remember about student work and behavior during the lesson? How did their actions match what you expected/hoped would happen?

How successful were the students in moving toward competency with the standard?

What do you think caused some of the students to not quite "get it?"

What did you notice that caused you to...?

What did you learn from this teaching and/or conferencing experience that will influence your future thinking and planning?

Observing One Another
in the Act of Teaching

Whether our purpose is "peer coaching" or "peer poaching," the act of "public teaching" promotes professional growth for all parties. When we know that a colleague is going to observe us, we are more thoughtful before we teach, while we teach, and after we teach. As if that was not a big enough payoff in and of itself, the discussions we hold prior to and following shared teaching and learning experiences are extraordinarily growth inducing. A sampling of teaching behaviors we might want feedback around, or on which we might want to gather data, is listed below.

AREAS of FOCUS

- calling on patterns
- balance of positive and negative feedback (praise and encouragement vs. reprimand)
- body language
- clarity of directions
- communication of objectives
- wait time
- time dedicated to interactive instruction vs. time dedicated to administrivia, housekeeping, and discipline
- balance of teacher talk and student talk
- match of activities to the stated objectives
- frequency of checking for understanding
- strategies for checking for understanding
- checking for understanding with whom
- dealing with errors
- strategies for dealing with students who do not understand
- strategies for dealing with students who do not answer or participate
- physical movement around the classroom
- teaching to all three modalities
- teaching for global and analytical learners

Observing One Another
in the Act of Teaching continued...

POSSIBLE AREAS of FOCUS

- teaching to the multiple intelligences
- developmentally appropriate practices
- match of instruction to national, state, and local standards
- student choice and decision making
- Differentiation of instruction
- speech patterns (noting vague terms or qualifiers)
- feeling tone (fun *to* no fun *to* too much fun)
- feeling tone (level of accountability vs. high anxiety)
- communication of expectations
- efficiency of transitions
- cognitive transitions between activities and assignments
- examples, analogies, and metaphors
- isolation of critical attributes
- hooks to past experiences
- accessing prior knowledge
- use of 10:2 theory
- "withitness"
- percent of use of target language
- dealing with errors
- responses to student answers
- responses to student questions
- student questions
- level of questions (Bloom's taxonomy)
- student interaction
- dealing with interruptions (external)
- dealing with off task behavior
- teaching of social/collaboration skills

...and 50,000 others!

Fundamentals of Co-Teaching

Successful co-teaching relies on effective communication. Simple matters, if not clarified, can lead to misunderstandings that interfere with the co-teaching success. Before you co-teach, and throughout the process, be sure to discuss these and any other fundamental issues you identify.

Instruction and Assessment

What are students to know and be able to do, and how will they demonstrate that learning? When you are working together in a standards based classroom there must be a clear understanding of what standard(s) is the focus of the instruction. Adaptations around assessment for special needs students may require much discussion. Will rubrics or performance task lists be used? What flexibility is built in and what might be areas of contention?

Planning

Who is going to take responsibility for what parts of the planning? When does planning get done? Does it happen one year, one month, one week, or one day in advance? Who designs the tasks, the assessment, and the criteria for demonstrating competency?

Instructional Format

How will the lesson be delivered and who will deliver it? What will be acceptable additions or clarifications? Which option for co-teaching will you use? How will a wide array of resources be assembled and organized? Who will take the lead for what tasks?

Teacher Status

How will it be clear to you and the students that you hold **equal status?** For example, think about how to do introductions to students, parents, and others, titles to be used, which names are on the report cards, who calls parents, and classroom allocation of adult space (such as desks and chairs).

Noise

How will the sound level in the classroom be monitored and adapted? Noise includes teacher voices, instructional activities, noise of machines or equipment, student voices, movement, and environmental sounds.

Fundamentals of Co-Teaching continued...

Classroom Routines

What expectations does each teacher have for how classes should operate? This includes everything from headings on student papers to permission to use the pencil sharpener or restroom. **Equal status** means that each teacher has input into such decisions.

Discipline

What are the acceptable standards for student classroom behavior? What is absolutely intolerable for each teacher and what is okay some of the time in some situations? What are the systems for rewards and consequences for behavior?

Feedback

When will you meet to assess how the co-teaching arrangement is operating and how you will discuss both successes and problems? Identify timelines for feedback and the format of the feedback in advance.

Grading

What will be the basis for grades and who will assign them? A discussion of the effect of instructional/assessment modifications on grades is an important topic.

Data Gathering and Analysis

What data will you need to gather to make future instructional decisions? How will this data about the effectiveness of instructional decisions and about student learning be gathered and analyzed?

Teaching Chores

Who scores assignments and tests? Who duplicates materials, reserves films, contacts speakers, arranges field trips, corrects papers, records grades, and so on?

Pet Peeves

What other aspects of classroom life are critical to you? The issue for you could be the extent of organization of materials, the ways students address teachers, or the fact that it really bothers you when someone opens your desk drawer without asking. Try to identify as many as possible in advance.

Options for Co-Teaching

Many teachers think of co-teaching as one or two approaches to having two adults instructing students in a classroom setting. In fact, there are many ways to approach co-teaching. The single most important issue to consider in any co-teaching setting is that the teachers, the students, and all other interested parties must believe and act as if the two teachers are of equal status. With that given in place, any of these options can be selected to accomplish the identified objectives and tasks.

One Instructor, One Observer One teacher has primary instructional responsibility, while the other observes and gathers data on students, their performance, their interactions, and their behavior in general; each teacher can assume either role.

One Instructor, One "Floater" One teacher has primary instructional responsibility, while the other assists students with their work, monitors behavior, corrects assignments, etc. Each teacher can assume either role.

Station Teaching Teachers divide instructional content into two parts (e.g., vocabulary and content, or new concepts and review). Each teacher instructs half the class in one area. Both groups of students rotate through instruction with each teacher.

Parallel Teaching Each teacher instructs half the student group; the same content is taught simultaneously to all students though instructional methods may vary.

Remedial Teaching One teacher instructs students who have mastered the material to be learned, while the other works with students who have not mastered the key concepts or skills.

Options for Co-Teaching continued...

Supplemental Teaching One teacher presents the lesson in standard format. The other works with students who have difficulty mastering the material, simplifying, and otherwise adapting instruction to meet their needs, OR works with students who have already mastered the material to provide enrichment and extension. This option is often used when special education teachers and regular education teachers first work together.

Team Teaching In this, the most sophisticated form of co-teaching, the teachers collaborate to present the lesson to all students. In fully developed team teaching situations, the teachers are so comfortable with their roles, the content, and the students that they are able to pick up on nuances and read each other's signals so well that they essentially teach as one.

Finding the right formula(s) for co-teaching is like figuring out how to get a strike in bowling. It takes lots of practice, trust in the process, thoughtful alignment with the goal, and thorough follow-through by the bowlers...and the teachers!

Making the Most of Mentoring Relationships

Since we cannot possibly learn all we need to know about the act of teaching during preservice education, learning during the induction period must continue at an intensive level. Careful selection of mentors is an essential component of designing productive mentoring relationships. Whether you are identifying your own mentor, or deciding whether to become one yourself, include the following criteria in assessing the appropriateness of the choice. A teacher teaching a new grade level or a new subject area may need a mentor just as much as a beginning teacher.

Mentor teachers should exhibit excellence in classroom teaching by:

+ demonstrating strong content knowledge
+ having and using a wide repertoire of teaching strategies
+ using a wide range of assessment tools
+ being willing to give special attention to students who need remedial or compensatory help as well as to students who need enrichment
+ demonstrating success in facilitating high student performance and achievement

Additional attributes of successful mentors include:

+ a history of collegial interactions or an expressed desire to collaborate with other educators in purposeful ways
+ an appreciation for, and skills for working with, a variety of teaching and learning styles
+ assignment to same subject level/grade level
+ commitment to own personal growth
+ willingness to be reflective about own teaching decisions
+ strong communication skills
+ knowledge of adult learning theory
+ capacity to match interactions and responses to knowledge, skills, and trust level of mentee

Mentoring Relationships continued...

Interactions between a new staff member and the mentor depend on the needs of the new staff member and the purposefulness of the district in promoting collegiality as a value of the district. If collegiality is a value of the district, then the frequency, intensity, and quality of the interactions between mentor and new staff member should clearly demonstrate that value.

Potentially Helpful Mentor Actions

+ Introduce the beginning teacher to members of the administrative staff, teachers, and other school employees.
+ Go over all school routines, rules, and policies...especially the unwritten ones!
+ Take the new teacher on a tour of the school grounds...and even of the school attendance zone.
+ Escort and sit with the new colleague at faculty meetings and staff development opportunities.
+ Remember to include the new staff member in informal social gatherings...either in the lounge or outside of school.
+ Observe the new teacher and give feedback as appropriate.
+ Encourage the new teacher to observe other teachers who teach the same subject/grade and/or the same students.
+ Teach a demonstration lesson or co-teach in the new teacher's classroom.
+ Involve the new teacher in co-curricular activities.
+ Help the new staff member recognize and appreciate the knowledge and expertise he/she brings to the profession.
+ Guide the new teacher through state and district standards; share time proven lessons and assessments that are efficient and effective in moving students toward meeting the standards.
+ Assist the new teacher with identifying a wide variety of materials and resources appropriate for the content and the students.
+ Inform the new staff member of how to obtain audio-visiual equipment and supplies as well as how to obtain all other supplies.
+ Coach the new colleague in how teachers collaborate around special needs students, whether it be in an inclusion model or a pullout model.
+ Explain the system's teacher supervision and evaluation system and go over the criteria for teaching performance used in the district.
+ Hold regularly scheduled meetings/conferences...daily, at first, and then weekly.

Building Collaborative Teams

I. Not all groups are teams. A group must have **common goals and objectives** in order to become a collaborative team.

II. The study of **school culture** is important because it, as well as **individual belief systems** of team members, will have a direct bearing on team effectiveness and team activities at each school.

III. Because team development does not happen quickly or in a linear fashion, team members need to understand the **change process.**

IV. Because **meetings** are an essential component of any teaming situation, team members must become experts in planning, leading, and participating in effective meetings.

V. Team members should complement each other; that is, they should learn to recognize, seek out, appreciate, and capitalize on **differences in styles, skills, talents, and interests.**

VI. Teams need to constantly assess and work to improve **communication** within teams and with those "outside" the team.

VII. Teams, early in the development process, should put in place **systems for dealing with problems and conflicts** and for making necessary adjustments in plans and procedures.

VIII. Team success depends on the degree to which members' needs for **influence and parity**, as well as a **sense of competence and confidence** are met.

IX. Team members must **take the initiative** to share ideas and practices they value and believe will strengthen their efforts. They must also be willing to **give up some autonomy** to accomplish actions based on common visions and agreements.

X. The high levels of commitment, energy, and enthusiasm typical at the beginning of the teaming experience can be maintained only with **reflective practice, a balance of autonomy and interdependence, guidance, training, and support.**

Resources & References

XII
Resources &
References

References and Resources

Armstrong, Thomas. **Multiple Intelligences in the Classroom**. Alexandria, VA: ASCD, 1994.

Armstrong, Thomas, **The Myth of the A.D.D. Child.** New York: Penguin Books, 1995.

Arth, Alfred A. and M. Olsen. "How to Assign Homework." **Middle School Journal**. February, 1980, pp 4-15.

Aronson, Elliot. **The Jigsaw Classroom**. Beverly Hills, CA: Sage, 1978.

Ashlock, Robert. **Error Patterns in Computation.** Columbus, Ohio: Charles E. Merrill, 1976.

Avery, Patricia G., Jacqueline Baker and Susan Gross. "'Mapping Learning at the Secondary Level" **The Social Studies.** September/October, 1996, pp 217-223.

Bailis, Pamela and Madeline Hunter. "Do Your Words Get Them to Think." **Learning 85.** August, 1985, p 43.

Bean, T. W. and J. Peterson. "Fostering Readiness in the Content Areas." **Reading Horizons**. 21, 1981.

Bennett, Barrie, Carol Rolheiser-Bennett and Laurie Stevahn. **Cooperative Learning: Where Heart Meets Mind**. Toronto, Ontario: Professional Development Associates, 1991.

Beyer, Barry K. **Improving Student Thinking.** Boston: Allyn and Bacon, 1997.

Black, Susan. "The Truth About Homework." **The American School Board Journal**. October, 1996, pp 48-51.

Blachowicz, C. L. Z. "Making Connections: Alternatives to the Vocabulary Notebook." **Journal of Reading,** 29, April 1986, 643-49.

Bonk, Curtis Jay. "P254/M201 Course Packet of Notes." Bloomington, IN: Indiana University, 1995.

Bower, Bert, Jim Lobdell, and Lee Swenson (Teachers' Curriculum Institute). **History Alive!** Addison-Wesley Publishing Company, Melno Park, California. 1994.

Brain and Learning, The: Facilitator's Guide. Alexandria, VA: Association for Supervsion and Curriculum Development, 1998.

Breaking Ranks: Changing an American Institution. Reston, VA: NASSP, 1996.

References and Resources continued...

Brophy, Jere. "Occasional Paper #101." **On Motivating Students.** East Lansing, MI: Institute for Research on Teaching, MSU, October, 1986.

Buckley, Marilyn Hanf. "When Teachers Decide to Integrate the Language Arts." **Language Arts.** April, 1986, pp 369-377.

Burke, Kay. **What To Do With The Kid Who... .** Palatine, IL: Skylight Publishing, Inc., 1992.

Butzow, John and Carol Butzow. "Making Science Livelier with Children's Fiction." **Learning 88.** March, 1988, pp 50-53.

Caine, Renate Nummela and Geoffrey Caine. **Education on the Edge of Possibility.** Alexandria, VA: ASCD, 1997.

Caine, Renate Nummela and Geoffrey Caine. **Making Connections.** Alexandria, VA: ASCD, 1991.

Campbell, Linda, Bruce Campbell and Dee Dickinson. **Teaching and Learning Through Multiple Intelligences**. Needhan Heights, MA: Allyn and Bacon, 1996.

Canady, Robert Lynn and Michael D. Rettig. **Teaching in the Block.** Princeton, NJ: Eye on Education, 1996.

Carey, Lou M. **Measuring and Evaluating School Learning**. Allyn and Bacon, Inc.: Boston, 1988.

Clarke, John H. "Using Visual Organizers to Focus on Thinking." **Journal of Reading**. vol 34, no 7, April, 1991, pp 526-534.

Coloroso, Barbara. **Kids are Worth It!** New York: William Morrow and Company, Inc. 1994.

Collins, Cathy. "Administrators Can Increase Their Students' High-Level Thinking Abilities." **The Clearing House.** vol 62, May, 1989, pp 391-395.

Connors, Neil A. **Homework.** Columbus, OH: National Middle School Association, 1991.

Cooper, Harris. "Synthesis of Research on Homework." **Educational Leadership.** November 1991, pp 85-91.

Costa, Arthur L. Editor. **Developing Minds.** Alexandria, VA: Association for Supervision and Curriculum Development, 1985.

References and Resources continued...

Costa, Arthur L. and Robert J. Garmston. **Cognitive Coaching: A Foundation for Renaissance Schools.** Norwood, MA: Christopher-Gordon Publishers, Inc., 1994.

Costa, Arthur L. and Bena Kallick, Editors. **Assessment in the Learning Organization.** Alexandria, VA: ASCD, 1995.

Cronin, Hines, Richard Sinatra and William F. Barkley. "Combining Writing with Text Organization in Content Instruction." **NASSP Bulletin**. vol 76, no 542, March, 1992.

Cruckshank, Donald R., Deborah L. Bainer and Kim K. Metcalf. **The Act of Teaching.** New York: McGraw-Hill, Inc., 1995.

Curwin, Richard L. and Allen N. Mendler. **Discipline with Dignity.** Alexandria, VA: ASCD. 1998.

Daniels, Harvey. **Literature Circles: Voice and Choice in the Student-Centered Classroom.** York, Maine: Stenhouse Publishers. 1994.

Davey, Beth. "Think Aloud Modeling." **Journal of Reading.** October, 1983.

Deschenes, Cathy, David G. Ebeling and Jeffery Sprague. **Adapting Curriculum and Instruction in Inclusive Classrooms: A Teacher's Desk Reference.** Bloomington, IN: Blooming Publications and Seminars, 1993.

Dishon, Dee and Pat Wilson O' Leary. **A Guidebook for Cooperative Learning**. 1984.

Dreikurs, Rudolf, Bernice Bronia Grunwald and Floy Childers Pepper. **Maintaining Sanity in the Classroom.** New York: Harper and Row, 1982.

Educators in Connecticut's Pomeraug Regional School District 15. **Performance-Based Learning and Assessment**. Alexandria, Virginia: ASCD, 1996.

Edwards, Phyllis R. "Using Dialectical Journals to Teach Thinking Skills." **Journal of Reading.** vol 35, no 4, December, 1991, pp 312-314.

"Effective Mathematics Teaching." National Council of Teachers of Mathematics, 1982.

Ellis, Susan S. and Susan F. Whalen. "Keys to Cooperative Learning." **Instructor.** vol 101, no 6, February, 1992, pp 34-37.

Fogarty, Robin. **Designs for Cooperative Interactions**. Palatine, IL: Skylight Publishing, Inc., 1990.

References and Resources continued...

-------------------- **Teaching Skillful Thinking: A Staff Development Program for Educators**. Alexandria, VA: ASCD.

Farr, Roger. "Teaching Good Habits with Think-Alongs." **Educational Leadership**. November, 1989, p 94.

Forte, Imogene and Sandra Schurr. **The Definitive Middle School Guide**. Nashville, TN: Incentive Publications, Inc., 1993.

Frayer, D., Frederick, and H. Klausmeir. "A Schema for Testing the Level of Cognitive Mastery." **Working Paper No. 16**. Madison, WI, Wisconsin Research and Development Center, 1969.

Gardner, Howard. **Frames of Mind**. New York: Basic Books, Inc., 1985.

Gibbs, Jeanne. **Tribes: A Process for Social Development and Cooperative Learning.** Santa Rosa, CA: Center Source Publications, 1987.

Gilbert, Judy, Editor, with the Northern Colorado BOCES SBE Design Team. **Facilitator's Guide and Workbook: Common Ground in the Standards-based Education Classroom.** Longmont, Colorado, 1997.

Goleman, Daniel. **Emotional Intelligence.** New York: Bantam Books, 1995.

Glasser, William. **Control Theory in the Classroom.** New York: Harper and Row, 1986.

Good, Thomas L. "Research in Classroom Teaching." **Handbook on Teaching and Policy.** New York: Longman, pp 42-80.

Good, Thomas L. and Jere E. Brophy. **Looking in Classrooms.** New York: Harper and Row, 1987.

Gronlund, Norman E. **Measurement and Evaluation in Teaching.** New York: MacMillan Publishing Company, 1985.

Grossmen, Bonnie and Doug Camine. "Translating Research on Text Structure into Classroom Practice." **Teaching Exceptional Children.** vol 24, Summer, 1992, pp 48-53.

Gould, Stephen Jay. **The Mismeasure of Man.** New York: W. W. Norton & Co., 1981.

Gunter, Mary Alice, Thomas H. Estes and Jan Schwab. **Instruction: A Models Approach.** Boston, MA: Allyn and Bacon, 1995.

Harmin, Merrill. **Inspiring Active Learning.** Alexandria, VA: ASCD, 1994.

References and Resources continued...

Hart, Leslie A. "Don't Teach Them, Help Them Learn." **Learning.** March, 1981, pp 38-40.

Heller, M. "How Do You Know What You Know? Metacognitive Modeling in the Content Areas." **Journal of Reading.** 29, 1986.

Hierstien, Judy. **Interactive Bulletin Boards**. Torrance, CA: Frank Schaffer Publications, Inc., 1993.

Hightshue, Deborah, Dott Ryan, Sally McKenna, Joe Tower and Brenda Brumley. "Writing in Junior and Senior High Schools." **The Kappan.** June, 1988, pp 725-728.

Howe, Michael J. A. **IQ in Question: The Truth about Intelligence.** London, England: Sage Publications, 1997.

Hyerle, David. **Visual Tools for Constructing Knowledge**. Alexandria, VA: ASCD, 1996.

Hunter, Madeline. **Mastery Teaching.** El Segundo, CA: TIP Publications, 1982.

"Instructional Staff Development Plan for Diversity." **Seminar Handouts: Day Four - Special Education.** Fairfax County Public Schools, Department of Student Services and Special Education, 1995.

Jackson, Michael C. and Norman D. Anderson. "ROY G. BIV Never Forgets." **The Science Teacher.** The National Science Teachers Association, 1988.

Jacobsen, David, Paul Eggen and Donald Kauchak. **Methods for Teaching: A Skills Approach.** Columbus, OH: Merrill Publishing Company, 1989.

James, Jennifer. **Thinking in the Future Tense.** New York: Simon & Schuster, 1996.

Jensen, Eric. **Teaching with the Brain in Mind.** Alexandria, VA: ASCD, 1998.

Johnson, David R. **Every Minute Counts: Making Your Math Class Work.** Palo Alto, CA: Dale Seymour Publications, 1982.

---------- **Making Minutes Count Even More: A Sequel for Every Minute Counts.** Palo Alto, CA: Dale Seymour Publications, 1986.

Johnson, David W. and Roger T. Johnson. **Reducing School Violence Through Conflict Resolution.** Alexandria VA: ASCD, 1995.

References and Resources continued...

------------ "Student-Student Interaction Ignored by Powerful." **Journal of Teacher Education**. vol 36, July-August, 1985, pp 22-26.

Jones, Beau Fly, Annemarie Sullivan Palinesar, Donna Sederburg Ogle, and Eileen Gylnn Carr. **Strategic Teaching and Learning: Cognitive Instruction in the Content Areas.** Alexandria, VA: ASCD, 1987.

Joyce, Bruce and Marsha Weil. **Models of Teaching.** Boston: Allyn and Bacon, 1996.

Kagan, Spencer. **Cooperative Learning Resources for Teachers.** San Juan Capistrano, CA: Resources for Teachers, 1990.

Kletzein, Sharon Benge and Lynda Baloche. "The Shifting Muffled Sound of the Pick: Facilitating Student-to-Student Discussions" **Journal of Reading**. vol 37, no 7, April, 1994, pp 540-544.

Kounin, Jacob. **Discipline and Group Management in the Classroom**. New York: Holt, Rinehart and Winston. 1970.

Lapp, Diane, James Flood and Nancy Farnan. **Content Area Reading and Learning Instructional Strategies.** Boston, MA: Allyn and Bacon, 1996.

Lee, J.F. and K.W. Pruitt. "Homework Assignments: Classroom Games or Teaching Tools." **Clearing House.** vol 53, 1979, pp 31-35.

Larson, Celia O. and Donald F. Dansereau. "Cooperative Learning in Dyads." **Journal of Reading.** vol 29, March 1986, pp 516-520.

Lozauskas, Dorothy and John Barell. "Reflective Reading." **The Science Teacher.** vol 59, no 8, November, 1992, pp 42-45.

"Managing Resources for Learning." **Student Manual for X150.** Bloomington, IN: Student Academic Center, Indiana University, 1994.

Marzano, Robert J. "Fostering Thinking Across the Curriculum Through Knowledge Restructuring." **Journal of Reading.** vol 34, no 7, April, 1991, pp 518-525.

------------ **A Different Kind of Classroom: Teaching with Dimensions of Learning.** Alexandria, VA: ASCD, 1992.

Marzono, Robert J., Debra Pickering and Jay McTighe. **Assessing Student Outcomes: Performance Assessment Using the Dimensions of Learning Model.** Alexandria, VA: ASCD, 1993.

References and Resources continued...

Masztal, Nancy B. "Cybernetic Sessions: A High Involvement Teaching Technique." **Reading, Research and Instruction.** vol 25, Winter, 1986, pp 131-138.

"Mathematics Resource Project." **Didactics and Mathematics.** Palo Alto, CA: Creative Publications, 1978.

Mathison, Carla. "Activating Student Interest in Content Area Reading." **Journal of Reading**. December, 1989, pp 170-176.

McCarthy, Bernice. **The 4MAT System.** Barrington, IL: EXCEL, Inc., 1987.

McKenzie, Gary R. "Data Charts: A Crutch for Helping Pupils Organize Reports." **Language Arts**. vol 56, no 7, October, 1979, pp 784-788.

Morison, Kay and Suzanne Brady. **Homework: Bridging the Gap.** Redmond, WA: Goodfellow Press, 1994.

Murnane, Richard, J. and Frank Levy. **Teaching the New Basic Skills**. New York: Martin Kessler Books, 1996.

Novak, Joseph. "Clarify with Concept Maps." **The Science Teacher.** October, 1991, pp 45-49.

Palinesar, A.S. and A.L. Brown. "Reciprocal Teaching of Comprehension-Fostering and Comprehension-Monitoring Activities." **Cognition and Instruction.** no 2, 1984, pp 117-175.

Peresich, Mark Lee, James David Meadows and Richard Sinatra. "Content Area Cognitive Mapping for Reading and Writing Proficiency." **Journal of Reading.** March, 1990, pp 424-432.

Pigford, Aretha B. "It's What Happens After the Teacher Stops Talking That Counts." **Principal.** May, 1989, pp 38-40.

Rakes, Thomas A. and Lana McWilliams. "Assessing Reading Skills in the Content Areas." **Reading in the Content Areas: Improving Classroom Instruction.** Dubuque, IA: Kendall/Hunt, 1985.

Raphael, Taffy E. "Teaching Learners About Sources of Information for Answering Comprehension Questions." **Journal of Reading.** vol 27, no 4, January, 1984, pp 303-310.

Readence, J.E., T.W. Bean and R.S. Baldwin. **Content Area Reading: An Integrated Approach.** Dubuque, IA: Kendall/Hunt, 1995.

References and Resources continued...

Rief, Sandra F. **How to Reach and Teach ADD/ADHD Children.** West Nyack, NY: The Center for Applied Research in Education, 1993.

Rief, Sandra F. and Julie A. Heimburge. **How to Reach and Teach All Students in the Inclusive Classroom.** West Nyack, NY: The Center for Applied Research in Education, 1996.

Rodriquiz, Rely, Editor. **"Instructional Strategies for All Students." A Compendium of Instructional Strategies for High School Teachers.** Fairfax, VA: Fairfax County Public Schools, 1995.

Rosenshine, Barak and R. Stevens. "Teaching Functions." **Handbook of Research on Teaching**. New York: Macmillan, pp 376- 391.

Rosenshine, Barak and Carla Meister. "The Use of Scaffolds for Teaching Higher-Level Cognitive Strategies." **Educational Leadership.** vol 49, no 7, April, 1992, pp 26-33.

Saphier, Jon and John D'Auria. **How to Bring Vision to School Improvement.** Carlisle, MA: Research for Better Teaching, 1993.

Saphier, Jon and Bob Gower. **The Skillful Teacher.** Carlisle, MA: Research for Better Teaching, 1997.

Saphier, Jon and Mary Ann Haley. **Activators.** Carlisle, MA: Research for Better Teaching, 1993.

---------- **Summarizers.** Carlisle, MA: Research for Better Teaching, 1993.

Schurr, Sandra L. **Dynamite in the Classroom**. Columbus, OH: National Middle School Association, 1989.

Sharon, D. and Hertz-Lazarowitz R. "A Group Investigation Method of Cooperative Learning in the Classroom." **Cooperation in Education.** Provo, UT: Brigham Young University Press, 1980, pp 14-46.

Silver, Harvey F., J. Robert Hanson, Richard W. Strong and Patricia B. Schwartz. **Teaching Styles and Strategies.** Woodbridge, NJ: Thoughtful Education Press, 1980.

Slavin, Robert E. **Using Student Team Learning.** Baltimore, MD: The John Hopkins Team Learning Project, 1986.

Slev, Barbara and Annie Gottlieb. **TEAMWORKS! Building Support Groups that Guarantee Success.** Warnerbooks, New York, 1989.

References and Resources continued...

Smith, R. and V. Dauer. "A Comprehension Monitoring Strategy for Content Reading Materials." **Journal of Reading.** November, 1984.

Sneed, Laurel C. "Making Your Video Tell a Story." **Training.** September, 1992, pp 59-63.

Silberman, Mel. **101 Ways to Make Training Active.** San Francisco, CA: Jossey-Bass, 1995.

Stevenson, Harold W. and James W. Stigler. **The Learning Gap.** New York: Summit Books, 1992.

Sylwester, Robert. **A Celebration of Neurons**. Alexandria, VA: ASCD Publications, 1995.

Taba, Hilda. **Teacher's Handbook to Elementary Social Studies: An Inductive Approach.** Reading, MA: Addison Wesley Publishing Company, 1971.

Tierney, Robert J. and James W. Cunningham. "Research on Teaching Reading Comprehension." **Handbook of Reading Research.** 1984, pp 609-641.

Tierney, Robert J., John E. Readence and Ernest K. Dishner. **Reading Strategies and Practices.** Boston, MA: Allyn and Bacon, 1995.

Tomlinson, Carol Ann. **How to Differentiate Instruction in Mixed-Ability Classrooms.** Alexandria, VA: ASCD, 1996.

Tyler, Ralph W. **Basic Principles of Curriculum and Instruction.** Chicago, IL: The University of Chicago Press, 1949.

Verble, Margaret. "How to Encourage Self-Discipline." **Learning 85**. August, 1985, pp 40-41.

Villa, Richard A. and Jacqueline S. Thousand. **Creating an Inclusive School.** Alexandria, VA: ASCD Publications, 1995.

Wassermann, Selma. **Asking the Right Question: The Essence of Teaching.** Bloomington, IN: Phi Delta Kappa Educational Foundation, 1992.

Wiggins, Grant. **Educative Assessment.** San Francisco: Jossey-Bass, 1998.

Wilkerson, Rhonda M. and Kinnard P. White. "Effects of the 4Mat System of Instruction on Students Achievement, Retention, and Attitudes." **The Elementary School Journal.** vol 88, no 4, March, 1988, pp 357-368.

References and Resources continued...

Winebrenner, Susan. **Teaching Gifted Kids in the Regular Classroom.** Minneapolis, MN: Free Spirit, 1992.

Wong, Bernice Y.L. and Wayne Hones. "Increasing Metacomprehension in Learning Disabled and Normally Achieving Students Through Self-Questioning Training." **Learning Disability Quarterly.** vol 5, Summer, 1982, pp 228-239.

Wong, Harry K. and Rosemary Tripi Wong.. **The First Days of School.** Sunnyvale, CA: Harry Wong Publications, 1991.

Wood, Judy W. **Adapting Instruction for Mainstreamed and At-Risk Students.** Columbus, OH: Merrill, 1992.

Wood, Judy W. and John A. Wooley. "Adapting Textbooks." **The Clearing House.** March, 1986, pp 332-335.

Wood, Karen D. "Fostering Cooperative Learning in Middle and Secondary Level Classrooms." **Journal of Reading.** October, 1987, pp 10-18.

Wyatt, Flora. "Rethinking the Research Project Through Cooperative Learning." **Middle School Journal.** September, 1988, pp 6-7.

ASK Group
Consulting & Workshops

ASK Group is a division of Attitudes, Skills, and Knowledge (ASK), Inc. a Virginia based firm established in 1989. The Group specializes in educational leadership, instruction and assessment, supervision and evaluation, induction, school improvement, and systemic change. Members spend much of their time working with school districts, collaboratives, and organizations in California, Colorado, Connecticut, Illinois, Indiana, Kansas, Ohio, Maine, Maryland, Massachusetts, New Hampshire, New Jersey, New York, Pennsylvania, Texas, Vermont, Virginia, and Wisconsin.

Each summer ASK Group members make presentations at the Harvard Principal's Institute and the Association of California School Administrators (ACSA) Principals' Institute at UCLA. Additionally, ASK Group is proud to continue a long term collaboration with Madam Lau KanHow to provide annual professional development opportunities for educators from the Ministry of Education, Singapore.

ASK Group offers a wide range of workshops, seminars, and programs. Among the most popular programs are:

Instruction for All Students

The six-day workshop series entitled *Instruction for All Students I* is offered for districts who are serious about long-term multifaceted work around teaching and learning in a standards-based environment. The culminating exercise is the presentation of a standards-based unit of study developed in collaboration with colleagues and taught by the participants in their own classrooms. They present their units, student work, data about the success of the work and planned revisions in a peer review session.

For educators who have developed content mastery, extensive repertoires, and an understanding of their diverse learners and are, therefore, ready to go to the next level, a second six-day workshop series entitled *Instruction for All Students II* is offered. This series has the same purposes as *Instruction for All Students I* with an explicit focus on the differentiation of instruction so that all students are challenged to, and supported in, their efforts to achieve at high levels. The units developed, taught and peer reviewed are more sophisticated in that they include multiple pathways to learning.

**The ASK Group is a division of
Attitudes, Skills & Knowledge (ASK) Inc.**
2214 King Street, Alexandria, VA 22301 USA
voice: 1-800-940-5434 fax: 703-535-8502
info@askeducation.com www.askeducation.com

Leading the Learning

This six-day workshop series focuses on the administrator's, coach's, mentor's and teacher leader's roles and responsibilities in ensuring that the school is organized around a commitment to the achievement of high standards by all students. It addresses the role that supervision and evaluation play in promoting teacher growth and student learning.

The work is based on the belief system that it is not enough for observers and supervisors of instruction to know that the lessons being offered in the classrooms are "good" lessons they need to know whether or not they are the "right" lessons. Supervision in a standards-based environment calls for extensive knowledge and skill in helping teachers plan and pace their instruction using the guidelines set forth by states and districts.

This series is designed to focus on gathering data and giving feedback in ways that go beyond meeting contract obligations and actually make a difference in professional practice. The learning experiences include carefully selected professional readings, action research, collegial interactions, direct instruction, and practice in data gathering and analysis combined with shared experiences observing teaching episodes.

Supervision & Evaluation in a Standards-Based Environment

ASK Group members work with school districts to review, refine and reframe their supervision and evaluation systems to align with current best thinking around assessment and to structure the process to promote teacher growth and student learning. This facilitation work focuses not only on the development of criteria for performance for district leadership, school administrators, and teachers but also on the reasons WHY to engage in the process beyond contractual obligations and HOW to decide what data to gather and analyze and HOW to provide feedback and engage in data-driven dialogue around the impact of practice on student learning.

Why Didn't I Learn This in College?

Why Didn't I Learn This in College? is as a four-day summer institute or an on-going school year workshop series. This new offering is in wide demand across the country as part of induction programs for teachers new to the profession. The essential questions which guide the work are:
- What is a learning-centered classroom and what do I need to do to create such a learning environment?
- How do I translate "beginning with the end in mind" into planning and pacing for the year, the unit and the lesson?
- What are systems for organizing me, the learners, and learning environment?

Institutes or workshop series are being offered this year in Colorado, Illinois, Massachusetts, New Jersey, and Wisconsin. Contact the ASK Group to investigate setting up an institute for your new teachers.

In addition to the programs described above, The ASK Group provides customized workshops around such topics as creating a collaborative culture/professional learning community, active learning, differentiation of instruction, working with adult learners, and job-embedded learning. Check the website www.askeducation.com for more information about possible consultations and workshops.

Feedback and Sharing Strategies

As you have read, many of the ideas and strategies in our books come from teachers and administrators around the world. Please share with us your feedback about *Instruction for All Students*. Also, if you have a teaching strategy that you would like to share for possible inclusion in future books and publications please let us know!

_____

_____

_____

_____

_____

_____

_____

_____

_____

_____

_____

_____

_____

_____

Name _____   **Mail or FAX to:**

Title _____

School/District _____   **Paula Rutherford**

Address _____   **c/o Just ASK Publications**

City _____ State ____ ZIP _____   **2214 King Street**
   Alexandria, VA 22301

E-mail _____

Telephone _____   **FAX: 703-535-8502**

Fax _____

2214 King Street Alexandria VA USA 22301   voice: 1-800-940-5434
fax: 703-535-8502 info@askeducation.com   www.askeducation.com

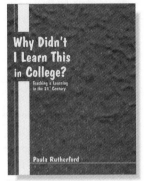

Just ASK Publications Order Form

Name _____

Title _____

School/District _____

Address _____

City _____ State _____ ZIP _____

E-mail _____

Telephone _____

Fax _____

> Make checks or purchase orders payable to Just ASK Publications.
>
> Mail or FAX to:
>
> **Just ASK Publications**
> 2214 King Street
> Alexandria, VA 22301
>
> **FAX: 703-535-8502**

Item	Price*	Qty.	Amount
Instruction for All Students by Paula Rutherford	$ 29.95	_____	_____
Why Didn't I Learn This in College? by Paula Rutherford	$ 29.95	_____	_____
The 21st Century Mentor's Handbook by Paula Rutherford	$ 34.95	_____	_____
Leading the Learning (3-ring binder) by Paula Rutherford	$ 59.95	_____	_____
Leading the Learning (bound) by Paula Rutherford	$ 34.95	_____	_____
ASK Poster Pack	$ 16.95	_____	_____
Overheads for *Instruction for All Students*	$250.00	_____	_____
Overheads for *Why Didn't I Learn This in College?*	$250.00	_____	_____
Results-Based Professional Development Models	$ 70.00	_____	_____
Operator's Guide for the Standards-Based Classroom	$ 45.00	_____	_____
Teaching Matters	$ 15.00	_____	_____
Points to Ponder: Volume One Video	$ 19.95	_____	_____
Points to Ponder: Volume Two Video	$ 19.95	_____	_____
Points to Ponder: Volume Three Video	$ 19.95	_____	_____
Points to Ponder: Volumes One, Two & Three DVD	$ 49.95	_____	_____
Data-Driven Instruction Video/DVD	$120.00	_____	_____
Success Factors in a Standards-Based Classroom Video	$ 75.00	_____	_____

SUBTOTAL _____

Please include 15% shipping and handling on orders under 10 units. Over 10 is 10% (outside U.S. is additional)   _____

TOTAL _____

*Contact Just ASK Publications for quantity discounts.

Payment Method

☐ Check or purchase order payable to Just ASK Publications.

☐ Visa, AMEX, MasterCard #_____Expiration Date _____

Name as it appears on the card _____

☐ Check here to receive information about ASK Group Consulting services and workshops.
I am interested in the following (optional):_____

Best way to contact me: _____

ASK, Inc. 2214 King Street Alexandria VA USA 22301 voice: 800-940-5434
fax: 703-535-8502 info@askeducation.com www.askeducation.com